RIGHTS OF PASSAGE

Equal Rights

VOL. I, No. 42.
FIVE CENTS

OFFICIAL WEEKLY OF
THE NATIONAL WOMAN'S PARTY

SATURDAY, DECEMBER 8, 1923

Drawn by Nina E. Allender

WOMAN'S WORK FOR WOMEN.
"The Sky's the Limit."

R·I·G·H·T·S
O·F
P·A·S·S·A·G·E
The Past and Future of the
———ERA———

Edited by

Joan Hoff-Wilson

for the
Organization of American Historians

Indiana University Press • Bloomington

To the memory of Alice Paul, 1885–1977

First Midland Book Edition 1986

© 1986 by the Organization of American Historians
All rights reserved

Manufactured in the United States of America

Library of Congress Cataloging-in-Publication Data
Main entry under title:

Rights of passage.

Bibliography: p.
Includes index.
1. Equal rights amendments—United States.
I. Hoff-Wilson, Joan, 1937– . II. Organization of
American Historians.
KF4758.R54 1986   342.73'0878   85-45073
ISBN 0-253-35013-1   347.302878
ISBN 0-253-20368-6 (pbk.)
OCLC: 12550018
1 2 3 4 5   90 89 88 87 86 `

Contents

Significance of the Defeat of the ERA

Foreword

WITH A FEW NOTABLE EXCEPTIONS,* most amendments to the Constitution submitted by Congress to the states for ratification, have been ratified, most of them speedily and without much controversy. Thus, the failure of the ERA in 1982 was one of the most important events in American political history.

*Although thousands of constitutional amendments have been introduced in Congress (over 800 before the Civil War and over 6,500 from 1860 to 1985), only twenty-two (in addition to the ten contained in the Bill of Rights) have received congressional approval and been submitted to the states for ratification. Of these, six (including the ERA) have failed to obtain the required three-fourths majority. The other five (in addition to the ERA) which have failed at the state level are: two proposed with the original ten amendments in 1789, one concerning representatives in Congress and the other with their remuneration; an amendment stating that no citizen shall hold a title of nobility without the consent of Congress (introduced in 1810); an amendment, introduced in 1861, that would have limited Congress's ability to abolish slavery through the amendment process; the Child Labor Amendment of 1924; and most recently, one giving representation to the District of Columbia. The average time required to ratify the existing twenty-six amendments to the U.S. constitution was seventeen months.

Significantly, the socioeconomic movements that resulted in congressional approval and ultimately state ratification of some of the more controversial amendments took decades. For example, the temperance movement began in 1811, the Prohibition party in 1864; over one hundred years in the case of the former and over fifty years in the case of the latter *before* Congress approved the Prohibition (Eighteenth) Amendment and it was ratified by the states. It took fifty-seven years from its first introduction in the House and a Civil War before Congress approved the Thirteenth Amendment freeing blacks from slavery. If one dates the beginning of the suffrage movement from the 1848 Seneca Falls Convention, seventy-two years elapsed before passage of the Nineteenth Amendment in 1920, and forty-nine years between the initial introduction of the Equal Rights Amendment in 1923 and congressional approval in 1972, or a total of fifty-nine years before its defeat in 1982, after a three-year extension of the original time limit. For more legal and political details about the reasons behind the amendment process and why some attempts to alter the constitution fail and others succeed, see Mary Frances Berry, *Why ERA Failed* (Bloomington: Indiana University Press, forthcoming).

—Editor's note.

· vii ·

The lively essays in this book (many of them were originally published in the OAH *Newsletter*) constitute one of the first attempts to deal with what will remain a controversial subject. Although the essays vary in tone, and although all of them are polemical in the best sense of that world, they make it very clear why an amendment which seemed to enjoy overwhelming popular support failed. That failure sheds bright light on all aspects of American politics and culture in the 1970s and 1980s. Hence, these essays, which open a window onto the very soul of the people of the United States toward the end of this century, are a significant contribution to the literature of recent American history.

The Organization of American Historians, which is dedicated to the promotion of the study of the history of the United States, is pleased to sponsor the publication of this book on the Equal Rights Amendment. The views of the authors are, of course, their own, and not necessarily those of the members of the association. But whether the readers of this book agree with the authors or not, they cannot fail to be fascinated and challenged by reading these essays about the significance of the defeat of the Equal Rights Amendment. Nor can they fail to learn a lot about the contemporary American political process as it operates on its most important level.

Arthur S. Link, President, 1984–1985
Organization of American Historians

Acknowledgments

A LITTLE OVER HALF of the essays on the Equal Rights Amendment in this collection originally appeared as short pieces in the quarterly Organization of American Historians *Newsletter* for a two-year period beginning in 1982, immediately following the defeat of the Twenty-seventh Amendment. Kathryn Caras, who was then a Ph.D. candidate, and Elizabeth Rogers, an M.A. student at Indiana University, initially copy edited and entered the articles published in the *Newsletter:* those by Amelia R. Fry, Jane DeHart-Mathews and Donald Mathews, Berenice A. Carroll, and Elizabeth Pleck.

Subsequently, I solicited other essays to give a broader picture of the reasons behind, and significance of, this latest determined effort to include women by gender in the federal Constitution. Dr. Caras initially edited these additional essays, as well. Moreover, many of the original *Newsletter* pieces were expanded or modified for publication in this collection. William Bishel, an Indiana University Ph.D. candidate, coordinated much of the final copy editing and organization of both sets of essays, particularly with respect to the incorporation of new material into the one on Alice Paul by her biographer Amelia R. Fry. As usual, the entire staff at OAH national headquarters in Bloomington provided a supportive atmosphere for all those who worked on various aspects of this OAH project.

In addition, I want to think Edie Mayo, Curator and Supervisor of the Division of Political History at the Smithsonian's National Museum of American History, for providing me with the entire collection of the illustrations on the covers of the National Woman's Party publication *Equal Rights;* pro- and anti-

ERA cartoons, some of which were donated by the Eagle Forum; and other memorabilia about the ERA campaign. Robin Morgan, who employed the term "Rights of Passage" first in a *Ms.* magazine article and then as a chapter title in her 1977 book *Going Too Far,* graciously consented to its use for these essays. My thanks also go to Constance Ashton Meyer, who compiled the various textual versions of the ERA, riders to it, and substitutes for it, which appear in the Appendix.

Finally, Arthur Link, as president of the OAH from April 1984 until April 1985, and the OAH executive board supported this publication. We all hope it will prove a useful tool for high school and college instructors who want to analyze for, and discuss with, their students the amendment, which will be remembered as the most controversial one of the last half of the twentieth century, regardless of whether it is ever ratified.

It is fitting that these essays should appear in 1985—the centenary of the birth of Alice Paul, author of the original 1923 ERA.

Joan Hoff-Wilson

Joan Hoff-Wilson

Introduction

EVEN IF THE EQUAL RIGHTS AMENDMENT is never resurrected and ratified, it will remain the symbol of the Second Women's Movement just as the suffrage amendment has been for the First Women's Movement. The ERA's defeat in 1982 perpetuates the condition of unequal constitutional status which generations of women have experienced because of their being omitted from the federal Constitution and the Bill of Rights. When the Founding Fathers translated the masculine system of justice based on eighteenth-century common-law concepts of liberty, justice, and equality into American constitutionalism, they simply confirmed that they were patriarchal products of their time—nothing more and nothing less. Consequently, most of the improvements in the legal status of American women have represented transgressions of traditional English common law.

In reviewing the legal status of U.S. women for any period, the words of Elizabeth Cady Stanton invariably come to mind. She and Susan B. Anthony discovered after the Civil War that women would have to organize separately from men to obtain their civil liberties. In the *History of Women Suffrage,* Stanton wrote:

> We thoroughly comprehended for the first time and saw as never before, that only from woman's standpoint could the battle be successfully fought, and victory secured. . . . But standing alone we learned our power; we repudiated man's counsel's forevermore; and solemnly vowed that there should never be another season of silence until woman had the same rights everywhere on this green earth as man.

Her words were as true for the First Women's Movement, which arose out of female dissatisfaction with former male abolitionists following the Civil War, as they are for the Second Women's Movement, which arose, in part, out of a not-so-dissimilar female dissatisfaction with the male-dominated civil rights and antiwar organizations in the late 1960s. Both represented significant attempts by American women to achieve equality under the law with American men.

With varying degrees of intensity, this struggle for equal rights has been going on for almost two centuries—since the drafting of the federal Constitution in 1787. Consequently, several generalizations can be made about the legal and political status of women in the United States. First, the English common law, which is the basis of the legal system of the United States, naturally reflected seventeenth- and eighteenth-century attitudes toward women. Thus, in the broadest sense the history of the legal status of American women has been a two-hundred-year struggle to overcome the civil and political disabilities embodied in English common law. During that time, their constitutional status has passed through four distinct phases and is on the brink of entering a fifth one. In this two-hundred-year period, there has been more change in the last twenty years than in the previous one hundred and eighty.

The first period, which lasted eighty-five years, from 1787 to 1872, can be called simply one of constitutional neglect, because the Founding Fathers did not have women's rights on their collective minds when they met in Carpenters' Hall. Nor were the Federalists and anti-Federalists thinking about women when the Bill of Rights later came into existence during the battle over ratification. Both documents, however, were written in remarkable, sex-neutral terms. Neither document specifically denied equal rights to women. By their frequent use of the terms *persons, people,* and *electors,* the Founding Fathers left open at least the possibility that women might be able to qualify to vote at some time in the future. It was not until Supreme Court decisions following the Civil War specifically classified women as other than full citizens of the United States that the hope faded that they could obtain the same suffrage and other rights as men through state legislation and judicial interpretation. Moreover, state courts interpreted very narrowly the Married Women's Property Acts passed before and after the Civil War.

In the second period of their constitutional development, lasting from 1872 until 1908, courts and state houses stopped neglecting women and began to discriminate actively against those who wanted to vote or enter certain previously all-male professions such as law and medicine. By 1900 women had tried systematically to use the Fourteenth Amendment to improve their legal and political status—initially through the privileges-and-immunities clause, then through the due-process clause, and finally through the equal protection clause. Failing in almost every instance, they turned to political action, focusing primarily on suffrage.

Thus, the second period in the development of the legal status of U.S. women ended on a discouraging note, but with one principle well established which would reemerge in the third and fourth periods: namely, that women should have equal rights with men under the Constitution. This principle became symbolically embodied in the struggle for an Equal Rights Amendment to the Constitution from 1923 until 1982.

The third period in the development of the legal status of women lasted from 1908 until the early 1960s. Unlike the first period of constitutional neglect, in which women's rights were largely ignored, and the second period of constitutional discrimination, in which the courts actively discriminated against women's professional, political, and civil aspirations, this third period was characterized by a variety of Supreme Court decisions (originating with *Muller* v. *Oregon* in 1908) and state legislation aimed at protecting women, especially those in lower socio-economic strata, based on what are considered today to be very debilitating stereotypical views of women. Ironically, just as protective legislation began to be used to restrict job opportunities for females, the First Women's Movement succeeded in obtaining passage of the Nineteenth Amendment, granting the female half of the population the right to vote.

Obviously, U.S. women had more political, legal, educational, and economic opportunities by 1920 than they had had in 1865. But they still had not achieved equality before the law with men. During the fight for suffrage, questions of personhood, credit, wages, pregnancy disability, domicile and alimony rights, rape, marital battering, child custody—even the right of married women to retain their birth names—all had remained neglected or subject to legislation which varied capriciously from state to state. A second women's movement would not emerge to take up these issues until the late 1960s. From the 1920s through the 1950s, there was little congressional legislation that made gender a central issue. With the defeat of the ERA in 1982, the Nineteenth Amendment, ratified in 1920, remains the only successful attempt to include women by gender in the Constitution.

During these same decades, aside from cases involving minimum working hours and other protective legislation, there were few significant Supreme Court decisions involving women, and those that did usually limited female activites: for example, the right to tend bar and to serve on juries. Under the combined influence of the Great Depression and New Deal legislation, the Supreme Court reversed itself and finally granted minimum wages to both men and women, but some of that same federal legislation discriminated against married working women and encouraged wage differentials between male and female workers. From 1894 until 1971, state courts often maintained that women were not legally *persons* for political and professional purposes, because that term was synonymous with *male*. It took a 1971 Supreme Court decision, *Reed* v. *Reed,* to overrule an earlier 1894 Supreme Court decision, *In re Lockwood,* 154 US 11 (1894), which allowed states to confine the legal definition of *person* to men only.

The last twenty years (roughly 1963 to 1984) constitute a fourth period, in which U.S. women have experienced more improvement in their legal and political status—despite the defeat of the ERA—than in the previous two hundred years. This quantum leap began in the early 1960s with a series of congressional acts, executive orders, and guidelines issued by government agencies created to enforce affirmative action. The breakthrough began with the Equal Pay Act in 1963, Title VII of the 1964 Civil Rights Act, and two executive orders in 1965 and 1967 (nos. 11246 and 11375) prohibiting certain kinds of discrimination by federal contractors. It continued in Congress with Title IX of the 1972 Educational Amendments and a 1978 amendment to Title VII requiring employers to provide employee benefits for pregnancy-related disabilities. In 1981, Congress passed legislation allowing state courts to divide military pensions equally when long-term marriages ended in divorce, and in 1984 it approved legislation facilitating the enforcement of child-support payments and the collection of pension payments for women.

All of these actions have aided greatly U.S. women in their two-century battle against sex discrimination in the work place, in educational institutions, and in their roles as wives and mothers. Supportive Supreme Court decisions began to appear in the 1970s, but the record of the justices has not been as consistently favorable to the cause of women's legal equality with men as have actions taken by Congress, some presidents, and government agencies. Passage of the ERA would have provided a comprehensive vehicle for ending sex discrimination throughout the country. However, the ERA should not be viewed as a panacea. Its passage in 1982 simply would have gradually promoted legal uniformity in the treatment of females in statutes and under the law of the land in a way that no previous act of Congress, executive order, or Supreme Court decision can.

In the wake of the ERA's defeat, we are prone to forget that the amendment was not designed to change values—only legal status. Its purpose was and is to provide equality of opportunity through the Constitution and legal system for those women who want to realize full personal and professional expectations within mainstream America. Had the ERA been ratified, it would have been absolutely noncoercive when it came to individual life-styles, because its enforcement powers were directed only against state and federal agencies or public officials, not private citizens. Also, it would not automatically have changed public policies based on traditional views of women as primarily home-makers.

In fact, the ERA may be more important in defeat than in victory, as a symbol of how far women still have to go to obtain true equality with men in American society. Its defeat has forced advocates of civil rights for women to seek creative legislation and judicial solutions in their continuing struggle for full and equal legal status with men. It has already resulted in a greater questioning of public policy negatively affecting women, such as the lack of comparable pay scales and the incompatability of working and school hours for women in the labor force with children. The success of the Nineteenth Amendment lulled into complacency many of those in the First Women's Movement. Perhaps the failure of the Twenty-seventh will inspire those in the Second Women's Movement to continue to strive not only for legal rights but also for value changes which will affect the everyday lives of women; thus they will enter a fifth stage in their legal and political development.

Looking back on the last two hundred years of U.S. women's history, other generalizations are evident in addition to the fact that women have experienced at least four stages in their consti-tutional development. A second characteristic is that throughout the nineteenth and twentieth centuries, it is difficult to charac-terize women's legal and political status as one of steady pro-gression. Rather, the pattern exhibited has been one of ups and downs depending on complex socioeconomic and political con-ditions. (One of the latest "downs," obviously, was the defeat of the ERA in 1982 and the decline of momentum at the state and local levels of drives to make laws more sex-neutral.)

Third, in several major instances our female ancestors have appeared to make major political or legal advances only to find those gains not institutionalized or accompanied by other rights to guarantee gender-neutral interpretation and enforcement. Often that occurred because improvement in the legal or political status of women came for reasons unrelated to their own liberation or freedom, that is, for conservative or anti-feminist reasons. Consequently, such statutory improvements in status did not necessarily reflect any basic change in society's paternalistic attitudes toward women. In the nineteenth century, good examples of increased contractual and fiduciary rights for women, resulting from an alliance of conservative forces, are the Married Women's Property Acts. Their conservative political origins encouraged the courts to resist any liberating interpretation of this kind of legislation. Alliances with conservative groups also accounted in part for passage of the Suffrage Amendment in 1920, and should have instructed those designing the strategy for passage of the ERA fifty years later.

Fourth, there has been a subtle interaction between the political and legal activities of U.S. women reformers since the Civil War. It is now possible to trace how the legislative and litigious activities of female activists varied in intensity depending upon their perception of their legal status at any given time. In fact, I would argue that to the degree the courts discouraged changes in female legal status, women often responded by taking political action as a form of compensation, and vice versa. Between 1872 and 1900, the Supreme Court not only denied women the right to vote and to practice law under certain conditions, it also more fundamentally questioned whether they were even "persons" under the law. Faced with such massive legal defeats, women reformers in the late nineteenth century took compensatory political action by organizing around the issue of suffrage.

Compensatory political actions, such as suffrage, typically *required* and *acquired* more conservative support than some of the more radical litigation in which women engaged in the late nineteenth century. This "seesaw" pattern continued into the twentieth century, as women took up such issues as protective legislation and the Equal Rights Amendment, as well as a series of court cases to overcome the debilitating effects of certain Supreme Court decisions stemming from the late nineteenth century. Until the 1960s, however, their legal efforts were unsuccessful except for brief periods of activity during the Progressive Era and New Deal. As a result, many women entered the mainstream political process from 1920 to 1960 as both Republicans and Democrats—in part because they made so little progress through litigation.

A similar, but more complicated, relationship between litigation and legislation has developed during the dramatic improvement in the position of women in American society which has taken place in the last twenty years. A more complicated relationship between the political and legal efforts of women exists today, especially since the defeat of the Equal Rights Amendment in 1982, as they try to determine which combination of strategies is better. As in the past, political actions often require more compromises and conservative coalition building than litigious ones, especially in the periods of cultural backlash following major wars in this century.

The lesson to be learned from this "seesaw" interaction is that when thwarted in the courts, women logically turned to political activity and in two major instances have organized to demand gender-specific inclusion in the Constitution. While the Nineteenth and Twenty-seventh amendments did provide those in the First and Second Women's Movements with invaluable organizational and consciousness-raising experiences, many turned the goal of suffrage and equal rights into illusory panaceas and talk about the power of a gender gap which has yet to significantly affect U.S. foreign or domestic policy, because women are too scattered among socioeconomic levels to vote or lobby as a single bloc.

Finally, it is also possible that many of the hard-won legal and political victories of women are examples of "too little too late." American women obtained the right to vote not in the nineteenth century, when it would have been truly significant in terms of grassroots Jacksonian politics, but in the 1920s, at the very time when electoral politics was showing the first signs of breaking down into the meaningless media-managed choices which are all too common today. Similarly, women obtained equal pay for equal work in the early 1960s and affirmative-action guidelines in the early 1970s, when the work ethic was being increasingly questioned and when there was less expansion in those sectors of the economy (such as educational institutions in which women were heavily concentrated) to make these advances in economic and civil status truly meaningful. Moreover, the Supreme Court may become more and more predisposed toward granting women full equal rights with men, just as some feminists have begun to question whether that should any longer be the most important goal of women as they anticipate entering the twenty-first century.

In the 1980s, some contemporary feminist historians, lawyers, and psychologists are beginning, more than ever before, to question whether U.S. women's long-sought-after goal of obtaining equality based primarily on individual, male rights stemming from the eighteenth century, should be pursued to its logical conclusion. Such women are looking back on two decades of dramatic improvement in their legal status and suggesting ways to recognize the limits of, and ways to go beyond, what has been called "liberal legalism," as they enter a fifth period in their constitutional development. In other words, certain feminists are evaluating the rapidly changing legal status of women between 1964 and 1984 in light of traditional views of progress, which stress women's obtaining the same rights as men, and nontraditional views, which stand the very essence of liberal legalism on its head by positing female, rather than male, standards for progress and justice. Consequently, the ERA may not remain the same symbolic issue for women in the last fifteen years of the twentieth century that it has been for many in the past fifty years, since it was first introduced in Congress.

This collection of essays represents an attempt to place the defeat of the Twenty-seventh Amendment in historical perspective. Whether one lauds or laments the defeat of the ERA, we can all learn from the reasons behind its rejection by legislatures across the country. The essays are divided by subject matter, beginning with the woman whose name will forever be linked with the ERA, Alice Paul. Then, several authors discuss from various perspectives the inability of ERA supporters to obtain the approval of the thirty-eight states needed for ratification. In the final section, the lasting significance of the ERA is analyzed from a legal and political point of view. Sometimes for quite different reasons, most of the authors agree that despite its failure, the ERA campaign was more than worth the effort.

Origins and Early Disagreements Over the ERA

Joan Hoff-Wilson

Introduction

PERHAPS THE MOST SIGNIFICANT ASPECT of the dispute between those who supported the Equal Rights Amendment in the early 1920s and those who did not is that it created a division between women reformers that lasted for fifty years. None of the original participants in this internecine struggle over the Twenty-seventh Amendment to the U.S. Constitution anticipated how long-lasting their dispute would be. After all, most of them had worked together to obtain passage and ratification of the Nineteenth Amendment. Although there had been numerous disagreements over tactics within the National American Woman Suffrage Association (NAWSA), the most serious occurred in 1913 with the formation of first the Congressional Union and later the National Woman's Party under Alice Paul's leadership.

When Alice Paul's followers finally broke with NAWSA, their tactical disagreement over how to obtain suffrage masked basic political, philosophical, legal, and linguistic differences among women that quickly surfaced over the ERA. Some of these fundamental divisions continue to the present day. While both Republican and Democratic women worked side by side for reform in the Progressive Era, by the time of the Great Depression and the New Deal, reform activity (except for some very prominent and wealthy Republican women supporting Alice Paul and the ERA) increasingly became identified with the Democratic women who followed first Florence Kelley and Jane Addams, and later Eleanor Roosevelt. Thus, the division over the ERA was, in part, perpetuated before and after the Second World War by partisanship, even though both parties endorsed the amendment beginning in the 1940s.

When certain New Deal legislation began overtly discriminating against married working women major female professional organizations came over to the ERA cause. During the interwar years, it was difficult to argue that there was a clear class or generational division among pro- and anti-ERA supporters, since the leaders on both sides were middle- and upper-middle-class women claiming they were acting on behalf of all women. Paul's followers tended to be younger than the antiratification women during the interwar years, but young women had become strong supporters of the ERA. In addition, there was an increasing tendency for professional and business women (often Republicans) to support the ERA, while until the early 1970s working-class women and male-dominated unions (usually Democrats) opposed it.

In addition to partisan politics and some class-conflict overtones, in retrospect, it is clear that the philosophical differences between these two groups of women reformers led to legal and rhetorical battles at home over protective legislation and the ERA, and at international conferences, the League of Nations, and later the United Nations over treaties that included broad guarantees for the equal treatment of men and women, especially with regard to independent nationality status and naturalization procedures.

By and large, those who originally opposed the ERA had been not only members of the suffrage movement but also members of the social-justice wing of the Progressive movement. That meant that long before winning the right to vote, these women had fought long and hard through litigation and legislation to protect working men, women, and children. Their later opposition to the ERA stemmed largely from their perception that it was based too much on the individual rather than on a group or social approach to reform.

Most historians of women have not shown convincingly how these two philosophically different approaches to reform led to two opposing views of equality and justice, something which continues to confound the debate over the ERA. Likewise, historians and political scientists have not adequately explained the dilemma which arises when women, like other disadvantaged groups, try to preserve a cultural or collective identity without being assimilated by the mainstream values reflected in pursuing equal rights. Nor have scholars clearly indicated how either a collective or an individualistic approach to reform relates to feminism. Thanks to the research of Karen Offen,* we now know that these two philosophical approaches for improving the legal status of women, in particular, and of reforming society in general, can be related to two distinct types of feminism.

Beginning in the nineteenth century, the most common brand of feminism in England and the United States was based on what Offen calls "radical individualism"; that is, it stressed obtaining the individual political and civil rights held by most men. The other kind of feminism she calls "familial" or "relational," because it is based on the "doctrine of equality in difference." It stresses biological as well as socialized differences between men and women and attempts to preserve these differences, not to ignore or to eliminate them with equal rights. Because they advocated a social or group approach for improving the socio-economic condition of the female half of the American population, those women who supported protective legislation in the early decades of the twentieth century most closely resemble those feminists Offen refers to as familial or relational feminists. With the exception of the United States and possibly England, this type of feminism is more widespread (and controversial) today in the Western world than the brand of feminism based on individual rights.

Consequently, it is possible to recognize something quite modern about those well-educated and often well-to-do women who emerged from the Progressive movement opposing the ERA. Their limited advocacy and application of collective justice

---

*"Toward an Historical Definition of Feminism: The Contribution of France," Center for Research on Women working paper no. 22, Stanford University.

should not be forgotten because it is so easy to criticize the long-term, negative consequences of protective legislation. Nonetheless, we have seen the "doctrine of difference in equality"—whether it be based on a separate-sphere argument or on an idealized and dangerously romantic vision of maternity, home, and family—co-opted too many times in this century alone by national and state objectives (e.g., in Nazi Germany, the Soviet Union, and China after their respective revolutions) not to be wary of the motivations of certain fundamentalist leaders among the New Right who are now espousing this version of "true" womanhood.

Despite all their shortcomings, the middle- and upper-class Progressive women who supported protective legislation spoke in Victorian terminology about morality, maternity, feminine sensibilities, and virtue that struck a chord in all women. Their language clearly indicates that they were trying to preserve a female haven—rooted in social and biological feminine behavior—a haven from male culture and male institutions. This peculiarly effective female form of communication was lost in the 1920s, according to Carroll Smith-Rosenberg,* ironically, in part because they began to use more modern male forms of communication. It has been only since the 1970s that attempts to create a similarly unifying language and to preserve the best of female socialized behavior have come back into vogue in certain feminist circles.

Smith-Rosenberg's fresh linguistic analysis now allows us to understand why the gap between these two groups of women reformers quickly became irrevocable in the 1920s. It was not simply that they disagreed over protective legislation and the ERA. Increasingly, Smith-Rosenberg points out, they spoke in "hostile languages" that reflected very different psychological approaches to their own sexuality, to reform, and to the question

---

*Carroll Smith-Rosenberg, *Disorderly Conduct: Visions of Gender in Victorian America* (New York: A. A. Knopf, 1985), pp. 252–305, 358 (n. 127).

of whether women should carve out for themselves independent, androgenous positions in politics, the professions, or the economy following the First World War. Until women begin to speak to each other in a common language, their impact on the domestic and foreign policies of the United States will remain marginal.

Amelia R. Fry

Alice Paul and the ERA

ALICE PAUL WAS EIGHTY-SEVEN when the ERA finally passed Congress in 1972. Though she had lived and worked for the forty-nine years of the campaign in the National Woman's Party (NWP) headquarters across from the national Capitol, she did not venture out to join the cheering women in the Senate that day. Instead, she saw the victory as presaging the amendment's ultimate defeat in the upcoming ratification. She believed that the bill contained fatal flaws—not in the language of the amendment itself (which she had drafted in 1922 and reworded in 1943) but in its enabling sections.

During those last months, Paul had lobbied frantically, sometimes almost alone, to change the flawed passages back to her original version. She had never allowed a time limit to be placed on "her" bill, but this one carried a seven-year deadline for ratification. Paul had always stipulated in the enforcement section of her draft that the power would reside in "Congress and the several States," but the final version omitted the reference to "the States" and left enforcement to the federal government—hardly a section that state righters would approve. Paul had warned that states in the South would be needed for the ratification total, and "the several States" would at least give the organizers a point in ideological debates. She had also pointed out that doubtful legislatures in states convening biennially could postpone a ratification vote for more than seven years just by assigning it to a study committee every four years. But no one—not even a majority in control of her own NWP—agreed that changing those clauses was worth postponing the vote in Congress.

A few generalizations can be offered about the methods and

strategies that Paul used in the long ERA campaign. First, the target was different from that of her suffrage campaign; after 1920 the campaign for equality was directed no longer at the party in power but at educating American women, at "changing their thought." Second, gender equality was pursued on all fronts in whatever public issue, national or international or local; but always the ERA was the central question. Third, Paul abandoned the direct militant actions and civil disobedience events for which she had become famous in the suffrage campaign. (For one reason, American women were too diffuse a target to picket or burn in effigy!) Fourth, she operated deliberately with a small party but a decentralized network that included NWP state chapters of varying sizes, and also with the chapters of other organizations, even some whose national offices were still opposed to the amendment. Fifth, she consistently based her tactics and arguments on thorough and meticulous research, which she generally directed. Sixth, she organized for state legislative reform, as well as a federal amendment. And finally, she used the international arena of the Pan American Union, the League of Nations, and the United Nations to press for codes and treaties equitable to both genders—the better to bring pressure on the United States to institute internal equal rights. This unique combination of strategies belies the usual description of Paul as a single-minded zealot intent only on a federal amendment.

When the Second Women's Movement arrived on the scene in the late 1960s, its participants' energies delighted Paul, but their scattered strategies distressed her. Although she never volunteered her views publicly, Paul felt that women, sometimes referred to as "New Wave" feminists, were creating opponents for the ERA by demanding rights for lesbians, legal abortions, peace in Vietnam, and school busing. Paul had spent half a century accumulating support for equal rights among liberal and conservative groups alike that had begun by opposing the amendment: the right wing, the Catholics, the radical left, states' righters, and, especially, organized labor and its allies, who saw the ERA as eliminating the special protections they had worked for on behalf of women. Few old or new feminists, including Paul, consciously anticipated that Phyllis Schlafly would emerge in the mid-1970s. However, Paul intuitively sensed that someone like Schlafly could coalesce the wide variety of groups that were offending in the burgeoning conservative climate following the end of the Vietnamese War.

Born in 1885 into a well-to-do Quaker family in Moorestown, New Jersey, Alice Paul attended Quaker schools until she went to Swarthmore College, and spent a year on New York's Lower East Side training in social case work. In the summer of that year, she worked on a project, sponsored jointly by the Women's Trade Union League and the Henry Street Settlement, to persuade labor unions to admit women. She also helped to form a milliner's union.[1] In 1907, Paul finished her master's degree at the University of Pennsylvania, and she attended the Quaker Woodbrooke Institute in conjunction with the University of Birmingham in England. Even though she had been disillusioned with social work as an effective corrective for poverty, she continued to use her training in various charity organizations in Birmingham and London. Paul also studied at the London School of Economics, lived by personal preference in London's East End among the disadvantaged with whom she worked, and engaged in six months of militant activities for the Pankhursts' Women's Social and Political Union in England and Scotland. By the end of 1909, she had undergone a series of jailings and imprisonments, hunger strikes, and forced feedings. It was this challenge that solidified her goal of women's rights as her life's work, and rightly so: it was very Quaker, quite progressive and reformist, and very Swarthmorean.[2]

Paul returned to the United States in 1910, finished her Ph.D. in 1912, and took charge of the federal amendment campaign for suffrage. That was a small committee in the National American Woman Suffrage Association, which soon split off to become the Congressional Union before becoming the National Woman's Party. Her strictly nonviolent program—parades, picketing, and burning President Wilson's words on democracy in urns with graceful pageantry and careful elocutions—though it differed greatly from the Pankhursts' actions, nonetheless resulted in incarceration, hunger strikes, and forced feedings.

Paul combined the Gandhi-like strategy of passive resistance and civil disobedience with mainstream political initiatives. She sent organizers out west (where some states had already enfranchised women) to campaign against all congressional candidates of "the party in power" on a one-issue platform: suffrage. Her aim was to create publicity for the cause amid competing "heavies"—such as war and peace—and to plant the threat of a possible women's cohesive vote in the minds of the Democrats. Whether or not the women's votes were, indeed, gender-conscious, Paul hoped that the *threat* of such would prod western Democrats to bring pressure on their more conservative southern congressmen to vote for the amendment. It was her first lesson in congressional lobbying.[3]

The two issues of states rights and women's role as homemakers have been central throughout the battle over ratification of the ERA. From its inception in the early 1920s, Paul had to face an added grievance: that an amendment for "blanket" equality for women would eliminate the protective legislation which for years reformers—including Paul and many members of her NWP Council—had sought for female industrial workers. For two years, Paul made determined efforts to keep the NWP neutral on the issue of protectionism while she worked to get other associations to agree on a construing clause which would exempt the amendment from changing any industrial protections for women.

But this conciliatory period between Paul and the protectionists ended in early 1922 when the National Consumers' League, led by former NWP Council member Florence Kelley, decided to oppose an ERA, and when the National Women's

Trade Union League gathered fifty representatives of women's groups to oppose a blanket bill even *with* the safeguarding clause. Prominent in opposition to the ERA were the Women's Christian Temperance Union, the National Mother and Parent Teachers' Association, the AAUW, the National Council of Jewish Women, and the League of Women Voters, which had sprung from the National American Woman Suffrage Association so critical of Paul's militance during suffrage. Inside government, the Women's Bureau, led by Mary Anderson, was against the ERA because of Anderson's effort to promote industrial protections for women only as Department of Labor policy.

At the same time, Paul appointed a committee of thirteen female attorneys, headed by Burnita Matthews, to survey discriminatory laws in each state and to write corrective legislative packages for each, which NWP state chapters presented and lobbied for consistently. Sometimes a "blanket amendment" was included—with and without the construing clause. The Wisconsin chapter led the passage of an ERA *with* the clause on June 21, 1921, but there were to be no others. By the end of the 1920s, the women could point to about three hundred state laws changed out of the six hundred they had submitted or advocated in all the states, although some were rescinded by successively conservative legislatures or ignored by state justice systems.

In November 1922, the NWP Council overcame its months of indecision and voted to work for a federal amendment that could guarantee women's equal rights regardless of legislatures' indecisions. Although the construing clause was not dropped, ERA opponents made it clear that it was not enough of a concession to make them allies—possibly because they still had strong reservations about Paul's militancy from suffrage days.[4]

By the time the NWP had the ERA first introduced in Congress in 1923, Paul saw women in industry as chief among those she should convert to effective advocates for the ERA. Her NWP Industrial Council had at least four hundred women lobbying and organizing in the 1920s. Many were workers who had lost

LEGISLATIVE CHRONOLOGY OF THE ERA:

Journey through Congress, 1923–1983

1923   —ERA introduced, December 10

1924   —Senate Judiciary Committee hearings, February 7

1925   —House Judiciary Subcommittee hearings, February 4
—Senate Subcommittee hearings, February 6

1929   —Senate Subcommittee hearings, February 1

1931   —Senate Subcommittee hearing, January 6

1932   —House Committee hearings, March 23

1933   —Senate Subcommittee hearings, bills tabled, May 27

1936   —House Subcommittee favorable, first time ever, May 30

1937   —House Subcommittee favorable, June 16
—Senate Subcommittee favorable, December 18

"Neighbors—National Woman's Party: 'Glad to see you back. We are coming to call next week.'" cover of *Equal Rights: Official Weekly of the National Woman's Party,* November 24, 1923. Courtesy National Museum of American History, Smithsonian Institution.

1938   —Senate Committee Hearings, February 7–10
       —Senate Subcommittee votes, March 7
       —Senate Subcommittee refers to full Committee,
          April 6
       —Senate Committee sends to floor without
          recommendation, April 25
       —Recommitted to Senate Committee, May 5

1939   —House Subcommittee, favorable report, April 26

1941   —House Subcommittee favorable report, after
          rewording considered, August 14

1942   —Senate Committee favorable, first time ever, May 11
       —House Committee votes favorably, but never reports
          ERA to floor, July 22

1943   —Senate Subcommittee favorable, February 17
       —House Subcommittee favorable report, March 3
       —Senate Committee adopts favorable report for Alice
          Paul's revision of wording, May 28
       —Discharge petition fails in House, December 13
       —House Subcommittee favorable report with Alice
          Paul's wording, June 23
       —House Committee votes against favorable report,
          October 5

1945   —House Committee hearings, February 21–March 31
       —House Committee favorable, April 21
       —House places it on calendar for floor vote for first
          time, July 12
       —Senate Subcommittee hearings, September 28
       —House Committee strikes from calender, reports it
          back to committee, October 1

1946   —Senate Committee favorable report, March 5
       —Senate floor vote, first time ever, (38–35 simple

majority) for Alice Paul version, no riders, July 19

1948   —Senate Committee favorable report, April 29
        —House Committee hearings, favorable report,
        March 14–June 1

1949   —Senate Committee favorable report, March 22

1950   —Senate passed by a two-thirds majority with Hayden
        rider (65–19), January 25
        —Discharge by petition to floor of House fails,
        March 6

1951   —Senate Committee favorable and Hayden rider
        attached, May 23

1953   —Senate Committee favorable, Alice Paul version,
        May 4
        —Senate passes with Hayden rider by a two-thirds
        majority, (73–11), July 16

1956   —Senate Committee hearings, April 11 and 12
        —Senate Committee favorable, May 14

1957   —Senate Committee favorable without riders,
        August 5
        —Senate Committee sends to Senate without any
        amendments but vote not called, August 27

1959   —Senate Committee favorable, no riders, May 20

1960   —Senate considers and votes to add rider, bill sent
        back to committee, July 2

1962   —Senate Committee rejects riders, gives favorable
        report to Alice Paul's wording, September 28

1964   —Senate Committee favorable report to Alice Paul's
        wording, no riders, September 14

1967 to —Over 140 ERA bills submitted in House, fewer in

1968   Senate, no action

1969   —Senate Subcommittee hearings, favorable report,
           May 5–7

1970   —Discharge petition from House, July 20
           —ERA passes House with two-thirds majority (352–
           15), no riders but seven-year ratification clause and
           "Congress and the several states" enforcement,
           August 10
           —Senate Committee hearings, many riders,
           September 9–15
           —From House to Senate where riders are attached,
           but no vote taken, October

1971   —House Subcommittee hearings, March 24–25,
           March 31–April 5
           —Voted out by Subcommittee with debilitating riders,
           June 4
           —Majority of full House Committee reports ERA
           with debilitating riders, June 22
           —Sent to House floor, July 14
           —Senate puts ERA on calendar but action postponed
           until 1972, September 8
           —On floor, House strips bill of riders, passes Alice
           Paul's ERA (354–24), more than two-thirds majority,
           first time ever, October 12

1972   —Senate Subcommittee reports ERA out with no
           riders, Alice Paul's wording, February 29
           —Senate passes ERA (84–8), Alice Paul's wording, but
           with seven-year limitation in ratification section and
           States omitted in enforcement clause, March 22

1972 to   —Thirty-five states ratify, three short of two-thirds
1977   necessary

1983   —ERA reintroduced into House

their jobs to men when employers did not want to pay the higher
minimum wage to women or to institute women-only protection
policies. Paul had come to believe that the first step for economic
transformation of women's oppression should be constitutional
protection against legalized inequality, and the organizers from
her industrial council were women who agreed and viewed
protections as an obstacle to employment in general, and economic advancement in particular. Paul, while born into an upper-middle-class family, as a Quaker social worker had seen
women barred from labor unions, denied job opportunities that
required night work, and denied the right to decide for themselves whether they wanted to take a job which required the
lifting of twenty-pound objects or being paid lower wages. At the
root of her decision to drop the construing clause and to oppose
protectionism was her belief that women should be treated as
individuals under the law just as men were, not as a class subject
to mass governmental regulation. The ERA would do away with
this underlying across-the-board inequality that permeated so
much of women's lives. Once it was ratified, "then," Paul would
say, "we shall see." Each woman would be free to exercise her
autonomy if she chose, and to choose her own life style, her role
in the family, and her work.[5]

Paul believed that women were, indeed, different from men;
that they were the nurturers and peacemakers and men the
hunters and warriors. But she held that this difference was
irrelevant to the question of equality in a democracy, and on this
principle she built her pro-ERA arguments.

Her policy of networking through other organizations began
in 1921 and continued throughout her life. The period immediately following World War I was one of decline for reform
groups generally, but the damaging effects on Paul's organizational capabilities through the shrinking NWP were not severe;
her connections with other federations of women were growing.
"Our membership was always very tiny," she explained. "We
thought the easiest way to get the Amendment through was to

try to get each of the national organizations to come out for it with its membership, not try to build up a duplicate membership of our own."[6]

During the Great Depression and the New Deal period, from the late 1920s to the late 1930s, Paul strengthened her network and leadership on behalf of obtaining equal nationality rights for women by cooperation with the League of Women Voters (LWV) for passage of the Cable Act in 1934. This statute gave married women U.S. citizenship independent of their husband's nationality status. During the same time that a group of influential Democratic women (many of them ardent supporters of protective legislation and opposed to the ERA) was influencing the social welfare policies of the New Deal under Eleanor Roosevelt's leadership, Paul provided space in NWP headquarters for a coalition of workers from such anti-ERA organizations as the Consumers' League and the League of Women Voters during their futile struggle to prevent passage of Section 213 of the Federal Economy Act, which barred both spouses from working for the federal government at the same time.[7] The NWP's Industrial Council and its ballooning Government Workers' Council led a similar coalition in an attack on New Deal legislation as one National Relief Administration code after another appeared with discriminatory provisions against women. In the process, more women were converted to the ERA movement.

May 30, 1936 was a milestone day: the House Judiciary subcommittee made its first favorable report to the parent committee. More groups than ever before testified with the Woman's Party for the ERA at the hearings. The following year, both House and Senate subcommittees gave it favorable reports, and in 1938 more extensive hearings took place. By this time, the National Business and Professional Women's clubs, the National Federation of Colored Women, the Women's International League for Peace and Freedom, and several national professional associations had put their weight behind Alice Paul and her blanket amendment. Paul instructed her state and national lieutenants to use the services of members and chapters of other organizations. On the practical level, labor regulations, which applied only to women and often restricted their employment in the name of protection, suffered a setback when the 1938 Fair Labor Standards Act, which applied to men and women equally, was passed. Although the Supreme Court upheld this legislation in 1941, the AFL and CIO continued to oppose the ERA until the early seventies on the grounds of protectionism.

When most protectionist laws were suspended during World War II to allow women to take the place of men in wartime industries, Paul thoroughly enjoyed the serious consideration that the ERA received in congressional committees. In a flurry of rewordings of the amendment, Paul's version (which is the present version) was adopted by the Senate committee, and more hearings led to a vote on the Senate floor in 1946. It passed by three votes, not enough for the required two-thirds majority, partly because of a surprise floor-call vote. Paul and her small group of lobbyists had such short notice that they had only minutes to see that all pro-ERA senators were in the Senate. When the vote was taken, eighteen senators sympathetic to the amendment were not yet in the chamber.[8]

The post-World War II years are usually identified by contemporary feminists as years of the "doldrums," the back-to-the-kitchen mystique in the suburbs. In the late 1940s, the NWP suffered from dwindling membership, in part because of an internecine fight for control of the party. A lawsuit in 1949 settled the matter in Paul's favor, and she immediately tried to attract new members and cooperate with more women's groups in the early 1950s, but with limited success. In addition, the Hayden and other riders consistently appended by ERA opponents in the 1940s and 1950s threatened the amendment's effectiveness and precipitated emergency lobbying just to keep it alive in committee. In the House, the head of the Judiciary Committee, Emanuel Celler, kept it in his "bottom drawer" the entire period he chaired the committee, 1951–1965. As early as 1956, the number of organizations of national scope that Paul could list as ERA endorsers had grown to twenty-eight, and on January 21, 29 senators and 208 House members were sponsoring the resolution.[9]

Paul believed that an international equal rights treaty, if ratified by the United States, would take precedence over internal domestic law under Article 4 of the Constitution. (Just before she received her doctorate of law, the Supreme Court, in the 1927 landmark decision *Holland* v. *Missouri,* upheld this interpretation.) So in the 1930s she took her battle for equal rights to the League of Nations headquarters at the Hague. She also created an NWP-dominated Inter-American Commission for Women, which became a part of the Pan American Union, and then directed a research project of all nationality laws in the Western Hemisphere and succeeded in getting an Equal Nationality Treaty signed by the participating governments in the 1933 Pan-American Conference. In addition, four Latin American states actually signed an Equal Rights Treaty at this conference. She carried these same efforts to the Conference on Codification of International Law at the Hague in 1930. Until the exigencies of war in 1941 prevented such travel, she commuted at least once a year to the League of Nations to lead her expanding network of international women's organizations, ultimately creating the Women's Consultative Committee.

Paul worked with her friend Doris Stevens to prevent or postpone passage of discriminatory international laws and also led a survey of nationality laws for the League of Nations similar to the multivolume opus she had produced for the Pan American Union. When she and Stevens lost control of the Inter-American Commission for Women in 1938, Paul engineered a discussion of the Equal Rights Treaty on the floor of the League Assembly just before World War II exploded. By that time, she also had organized the World Woman's Party as an offshoot of the NWP and rented a Villa Bartholoni near the league's headquarters in Geneva, Switzerland. This villa quickly filled with

feminists and liberal refugees of various countries, women fleeing from Hitler's advance. Paul's work was devoted largely to an
attempt to get them into the United States, but her meetings of
the Equal Rights International and World Woman's Party continued until she had to leave in 1941.[10]

Following the end of the Second World War, Paul and her
various domestic and foreign allies, which now included some
influential Third World women, turned back to the international
arena by lobbying at the newly created United Nations. They
ultimately succeeded in persuading Eleanor Roosevelt, who
chaired the UN Human Rights Commission, to substitute the
word *people* for *men* in the phrase "All men are created equal"
when drafting the now-famous Universal Declaration of Rights.

Undaunted by congressional recalcitrance at home on the
ERA throughout the 1950s, at the age of seventy-nine, Alice
Paul, helped by less than a handful of NWP faithfuls, put together enough votes from members of Congress with widely
varying motivations to get the word *sex* written into Title VII of
the 1964 Civil Rights Act.[11]

The New Wave of feminists organized NOW in the same year,
and Paul immediately joined. Martha Griffiths submitted the
ERA in the House—her first time as a sponsor. Representative
Emanuel Celler immediately blocked it. New Wave feminist
Betty Friedan wanted a new wording for the ERA and appointed a NOW committee of three, who came to see Alice Paul
at NWP headquarters. She convinced two of the three that they
should allow the old version to stand, because it now carried the
signatures of so many members of Congress, and that too many
years would be required to amass comparable support for a new
version. While the basic text prevailed, subclauses included a
seven-year limitation for ratification and removed "the States"
from the enforcement process. Paul fought both changes in
committee, but the Griffiths-Bayh version had too many sponsors for Paul's objections to prevail. It passed both houses in
1972. In Alice Paul's words: "We lost."

Momentum for the passage of the ERA in Congress came, ironically, on the eve of the end of the war in Vietnam, which would precipitate a broadly conservative climate opposed to socioeconomic reform. Nonetheless, Paul's aging and small band of first-generation supporters of the ERA dug in with sharper arguments, expanding networks, and more hours in the hall of Congress. This time they found eager allies among feminists organizing the Second Women's Movement. Few among this new and seemingly invincible coalition of women reformers, with the notable exception of the frail little woman who had started it all, anticipated that they were embarking upon a losing cause when in 1972 Congress sent the ERA to the states for ratification—forty-nine years after it had begun its tortuous legislative journey. (See Legislative Chronology of the ERA, pp. 13)

By 1972, Paul was almost alone, estranged from many in her own Woman's Party and perplexed about the many organizations and splintered goals of the new feminists. Although she used her telephone to activate key people in ratifying states, her failing health confined her to a nursing home. She died in 1977, knowing that the ERA would not be passed because of increased conservatism in the South and other parts of the country following the end of the war in Vietnam.

To assess Alice Paul's contribution to equalitarianism in women's history—or in human history, for that matter—one has to follow the trail of her influence beyond her party and into other organizations. A picture emerges of her handiwork, often behind the scenes in good Quaker fashion. But *there* she was—in Don Edward's office of the House Subcommittee, in New York or Minnesota or Louisiana legislative debates on equalitarian codes, in the chambers of the League of Nations and the International Labor Office, in working committees of the United Nations, on the telephone lines to groups opposed to the Civil Rights Act, in the proceedings of the Inter-American Commission for Women, even in amicus curiae briefs to the U.S. Supreme Court.[12] On the front lines, she led some of the most brilliant professional workers of her day, as well as industrial workers and government employees' groups. Her goal of educating successive generations of these women, by changing their attitudes toward equal rights, can, I believe, be said to have succeeded. Her political goal of an ERA is yet to be achieved, but she probably moved it a greater distance than anyone else—at least halfway up the mountain.

NOTES

1. Amelia R. Fry, *Conversations with Alice Paul* (an oral history conducted for the Regional Oral History Office, the Bancroft Library, University of California, Berkeley, 1972–73), p. 436.

2. Fry, *Conversations*, pp. 1–49; see also Alice Paul clippings collections, Newark Public Library, Newark, New Jersey; and Amelia R. Fry, "Alice Paul and the Divine Discontent," Proceedings, New Jersey History Symposium, 1981.

3. For a fuller treatment of this hypothesis, see Amelia R. Fry, "Alice Paul, Suffrage, Racism, and the South" (paper delivered at the Southern History Association Conference, Louisville, Kentucky, 1981).

4. I am especially indebted to Peter Geidel, "The National Woman's Party and the Origins of the ERA, 1920–23 (Master's thesis, Columbia University).

5. Fry, *Conversations*, pp. 271, 402–403; see also Alice Kessler-Harris, *Out to Work* (New York: Oxford University Press, 1982), chap. 7.

6. Fry, *Conversations*, p. 442. A glimpse of Fry's efforts to get other organizations to work for the ERA is provided in Helen Hunt West's "Progress Report" of the Congressional Committee of the National Woman's Party for July 16, 1938 (Helen Hunt West Collection, the Schlesinger Library, Radcliffe College). It is a typical example.

7. Susan D. Becker, *The Origins of the Equal Rights Amendment: American Feminism between the Wars* (Westport, Conn.: Greenwood Press, 1981), p. 149.

8. Fry, *Conversations*, p. 517; and Alice Paul to Helen Hunt West, August 8, 1946 (Helen Hunt West Collection, folder 9).

9. Helen Hunt West Collection, folder 14.

10. The papers generated in Geneva burned when the headquarters were closed that year, but correspondence exists in the National Woman's Party papers, Series VII in "National Woman's Party Papers, 1913–1974" (Microfilming Corporation of America). In the papers of the League of Nations, the records relating to Alice Paul and her committee are not microfilmed because they are on the committee level;

they are available only at the United Nations Library, Geneva, in the Archives of the League of Nations, 1919–1946. See especially files marked 3E/25712/25640 and 3E/2288/2288-XIII and 3E/21530/13900 and succeeding years. See Malvina H. Guggenheim and Elizabeth F. Defeis, "United States Participation in International Agreements Providing Rights for Women," 10 *Loyola Law Review* 1 (1976):1–71.

11. Carl M. Brauer, "The Prohibition of Sex Discrimination in Title VII of the 1964 Civil Rights Act," *Journal of Southern History* 49 (February 1983): 37–56.

12. Two examples of amicus curiae briefs submitted to the Supreme Court are *Adkins* v. *Children's Hospital* ZGI U.S. 525 (1923) and *West Coast* v. *Parrish* 300 U.S. 379 (1937).

Kathryn Kish Sklar

Why Were Most Politically Active Women Opposed to the ERA in the 1920S?

STUDENTS OF THE HISTORY of American women are often surprised to discover that the vast majority of suffrage supporters were opposed to the Equal Rights Amendment when it was first proposed in the 1920s. Why were groups as diverse as the National Women's Trade Union League, the General Federation of

"Women Must Save the Future Generation," cover of *Equal Rights: Official Weekly of the National Woman's Party,* March 1, 1924. Courtesy National Museum of American History, Smithsonian Institution.

Women's Clubs, and the League of Women Voters initially hostile to the ERA? Why did some of them remain hostile for decades thereafter? Why did most women reformers view the amendment's proponents as traitors to the cause of "organized womanhood"? Answers to these questions are important to a complete understanding of the history of the Equal Rights Amendment. They help explain not only why most politically active women opposed the ERA in the 1920s, but why they continued to do so until the 1970s, long after the conditions that generated their initial hostility had ceased to exist. As a strategy for understanding that hostility, this essay focuses on Florence Kelley, the amendment's chief opponent.

Opposition to the amendment had many sources within the ranks of those who supported woman suffrage. Some championed a more conservative approach to the advancement of women's rights, preferring piecemeal or gradual changes to the "blanket" approach of a constitutional amendment. Others objected to the cult of personality that developed within the National Woman's Party around the amendment's originator, Alice Paul. But by far the chief origin of resistance to the early ERA was the fear generated among opponents that the amendment would invalidate a wide range of labor and health legislation that women reformers during the past thirty years had struggled to obtain for American working and poor women.[1]

Such legislative efforts peaked in 1921 with the passage of the Sheppard-Towner Maternity and Infancy Protection Act, which sought to reduce the nation's high rates of infant and maternal mortality through the allocation of federal funds for health education at the county level. The amendment was doomed from the start, since only a tiny minority of women activists (primarily from elite backgrounds) were willing to jeopardize what most women saw as essential protections for female workers and for mothers.[2]

Although scholars have only begun to study the history of early opposition to the Equal Rights Amendment, it seems clear that many active opponents viewed themselves as participants in a class struggle to alleviate the oppression of poor women and children. Florence Kelley (1859–1932) typified and led this source of ERA opposition. Whereas most hostility toward the ERA in the 1980s tends to come from the political right, in the 1920s it was located primarily on the political left. Kelley herself was a lifelong socialist. As secretary general of the National Consumers' League from its founding in 1899 until her death in 1932, she was the single most powerful force behind the passage of child-labor legislation and hours and wages laws for working women.[3]

In 1953, U.S. Supreme Court Justice Felix Frankfurter wrote that Kelley "had probably the largest single share in shaping the social history of the United States during the first thirty years of this century," owing to her powerful role "in securing legislation for the removal of the most glaring abuses of our hectic industrialization following the Civil War." Even more important than the legislation itself, Frankfurter thought, was "the continuing process she so largely helped to initiate, by which social legislation is promoted and eventually gets on the statute books."[4]

The passage of social legislation was more difficult in the United States than in Great Britain and elsewhere. That was in part because of the power invested in the judicial branch of government, especially the U.S. Supreme Court, which in the late nineteenth and early twentieth centuries was very conservative. A fateful court decision in 1905 defined the vexatious terms under which American reformers had to lobby for social legislation in ensuing decades. In *Lochner* v. *New York*, the court ruled unconstitutional a state law limiting to ten hours the working day for those employed in bakeries. The rationale behind the law was that longer hours were unhealthy, tending to promote tuberculosis and other diseases, which were then passed on to customers. The court's opinion held, however, that hours could be regulated only when the worker himself was exposed to unhealthy conditions, such as in mines. Otherwise the terms of the contract between employers and employees could not be regulated.[5]

Eventually the court reversed this stand, ruling in *Bunting* v. *Oregon* in 1917 that state laws limiting working hours in manufacturing to ten a day were constitutional. The precedent for the court's 1917 ruling came in 1908, when in response to the *Lochner* decision, Florence Kelley and her allies successfully argued in *Muller* v. *Oregon* that the hours of women working in manufacturing could constitutionally be limited to ten a day, since sociological evidence demonstrated that women's health was injured when they labored longer than ten hours daily.[6]

Historians of labor legislation in the United States have noted that men tended to "fight the battle from behind the women's petticoats," since men benefited from laws passed to protect women, and since men's laws tended to follow the legal precedent set by women's.[7] That was true in other countries, as well, but nowhere so emphatically as in the United States, since in no other Western nation was it so difficult to obtain such regulations. In the 1920s, one-half of those employed in the steel industry worked twelve hours a day—longer than in any other nation except Japan.[8] Even though the eight-hour day was the single most popular goal of the labor movement in the United States as early as the 1880s, it was not established for all workers by federal legislation until the Fair Labor Standards Act of 1938—an act upheld by the U.S. Supreme Court in 1941. Thus, in response to the 1905 *Lochner* decision, Kelley and her associates in the National Consumers' League pursued a strategy of obtaining court approval of minimum-hour legislation for women and then extending that approval to cover men. She and her allies were almost as instrumental in the 1917 *Bunting* decision as in the 1908 *Muller* decision.[9] They used gender-specific legislation as a means of advancing class-specific goals.*

---

*It should be noted that while social reformers used similar statistical and gender-based arguments in *Muller* and *Bunting* to obtain minimum wages for women and men, the Supreme Court did not. Instead, the justices' concern for

Florence Kelley was extremely effective in organizing middle-class women consumers into groups that undertook political action on behalf of what they saw as the rights and interests of working women and children. By 1912 some sixty local chapters of the National Consumers' League had successfully agitated for legislation governing the labor of children in almost every state, and that of women in most states.[10]

Kelley's personal charisma and moral indignation over the oppression of women and children workers fueled much of this activity. During a 1908 visit to the United States, the German sociologist Max Weber found Kelley "by far the most outstanding figure" he and his wife had met; he learned from her "a great deal more about the radically evil things in this world."[11] In part Kelley's moral fervor came from her Quaker family background. As early as 1882, the year she graduated from Cornell, she published an article on the oppression of women workers, "Need Our Working Women Despair?"[12] In part her fervor was due to her knowledge of the "scientific materialistic" writings of Karl Marx and Friedrich Engels, which she translated in the 1880s. She developed a lifelong commitment to socialism in the 1880s and saw class struggle behind the exploitative practices of the sweatshop conditions in which women and children toiled long hours for pitifully small wages.

As a socialist, Kelley saw the power of the state as the logical means of ending such oppression. And as the daughter of one of

overworked men was based on the stereotypical views that they would not make good citizens, while overworked women would not make good mothers and wives. See Anne Corinne Hill, "Protection of Women Workers and the Courts: A Legal Case History," *Feminist Studies* 5 (Summer 1979), n. 14, p. 272. Rather than responding to the socioeconomic facts in these early protective legislation cases, Nancy S. Erickson has demonstrated that the justices relied on intuitive "common knowledge" about differences between men and women about what constituted healthy or unhealthy working conditions. See Nancy S. Erickson, "Historical Background of 'Protective' Labor Legislation: *Muller v. Orgeon*," in D. Kelly Weisberg, ed., *Women and the Law: A Social Historical Perspective* (Cambridge: Schenkman Publishing Co., 1982), vol. 2, pp. 155–86. The "Brandeis brief" statistical approach had more immediate impact on state legislatures than it did on legal interpretation before the Great Depression.

the most influential congressmen in the nineteenth century (William "Pig Iron" Kelley, who was elected to fifteen consecutive terms in the U.S. House of Representatives between 1860 and 1890), Florence Kelley knew that government was responsive to organized groups, especially those that represented the interests of capital. As she saw it, her contribution to the political process was to make government more responsive to the interests of laboring women and children.

Florence Kelley's success was based on more than her own personal charisma and background, however, for she was born into a generation of middle- and upper-middle-class women who constituted the first generation of college-educated women, many of whom did not marry and instead devoted their lives to much-needed social reforms. In the 1890s, a significant number of these college graduates joined forces in the social settlement movement. Living together in houses in the midst of urban slums, these reformers formed lifelong communities, providing one another with mutual support and supplying their society with an ongoing critique of the causes and consequences of urban poverty. In 1891 there were only six settlements in the United States; by 1900 over a hundred had been founded, and by 1910 there were more than four hundred. Thereby talented women were recruited into social reform in every American city.[13]

Jane Addams, cofounder in 1889 of America's most famous social settlement, Hull House of Chicago, was the best known of this group of college-educated women, but it also included many other activists who organized themselves and others to advance enlightened public policy. Hull House residents included, for example, Julia Lathrop, first director of the U.S. Children's Bureau from 1911 to 1920; Dr. Alice Hamilton, founder of the field of industrial medicine; and Grace Abbott, founder in 1907 of the Immigrants Protective League. In New York at the Henry Street Settlement, which she founded in 1895, Lillian Wald pioneered in the organization of public-health nursing. Florence

Kelley was a bridge between the settlements of Chicago and New York, since she lived with Addams in the 1890s and with the Henry Street group from 1899 until 1926. More than at any time before or since, settlements made possible the consolidation of the energies of women activists, vastly increasing their social and political effectiveness.[14]

Thus, when the suffrage movement modernized its tactics under the direction of Carrie Chapman Catt in 1910 and embarked on the last stage of its protracted struggle to bring women into the mainstream of American political life, other women were already well established in that mainstream. Viewing their causes as mutually beneficial, social reformers and suffragists joined forces during the decade before the passage of the Nineteenth Amendment in 1920. Votes for women would enhance the power of social reformers, while the reformers' social agenda strengthened the suffrage cause by providing concrete examples of the good that would flow from women's votes.[15]

Nevertheless, any coalition as diverse as the one supporting woman suffrage in 1920 was likely to break up when the single issue that tied it together was accomplished. Thus, even more surprising than the divergence of the National Woman's Party from the rest of the suffrage movement in 1921 was the solidarity that persisted among other elements of the suffrage coalition after the vote was won.

That solidarity was nowhere more visible than in the movement's opposition to what they called the "blanket amendment." By January 1923, the *New York Times* listed the following organizations in the amendment's "counterlobby": "the League of Women Voters, the National Consumers' League, the Women's Trade Union League, the Charity Organization Society, the Girls' Friendly Society, the National Council of Catholic Women, the Council of Jewish Women, the National Association for Labor Legislation, the Women's Christian Temperance Union, the American Association for Organizing Family Social Work, the

National League of Girls' Clubs, the Parent Teachers' Association, the National Federation of Federal Employees, and the
National Congress of Mothers."[16] Also opposed were the American Association of University Women, the YWCA, and the
General Federation of Women's Clubs. Only the National
Federation of Business and Professional Women's Clubs did not
openly oppose the proposed amendment.[17]

This remarkable unanimity among women's groups was partly
due to their reluctance to venture into new and more radical
solutions to women's inequality. To a considerable degree, however, it was also due to the momentum of social reform within
the suffrage movement that supported the enactment of special
protective legislation for working and for poor women. The
Sheppard-Towner Act was passed in 1921 as a result of effective
lobbying efforts of some twenty women's organizations combined under the umbrella organization of the Women's Joint
Congressional Committee. Many believed that such special legislation, as well as state mothers' pension laws and other protective
measures, would be invalidated by the Equal Rights Amendment.[18]

A solution to this dilemma was tried in the state of Wisconsin,
where in 1921 a version of the ERA was passed with a clause that
exempted all legislation designed to protect women. The
Wisconsin example failed to resolve the debate, however, because the Wisconsin judiciary was noted for its political liberalism and thus could not provide an adequate test of how the
amendment might be interpreted by the more conservative
federal judiciary.[19]

Meanwhile, the antagonism to the amendment by reform
leaders such as Florence Kelley was vastly increased in the early
1920s by the U.S. Supreme Court's consideration of the constitutionality of minimum-wage laws for women. By 1923, fifteen
states and territories, beginning with Massachusetts in 1912, had
passed minimum-wage statutes for women. Florence Kelley and
the National Consumers' League were the chief proponents of

this reform. In *Adkins* v. *Children's Hospital,* the U.S. Supreme Court ruled the Washington, D.C. minimum-wage law unconstitutional, saying that the Nineteenth Amendment demonstrated that men and women were equal, and therefore women did not need special legislation. Revealing the antilabor and procapital bias of the decision, the court wrote that "it should be remembered that of the three fundamental principles which underlie government, and for which government exists—life, liberty, and property—the chief of these is property."[20] Minimum-wage laws were crippled by this decision until the Supreme Court began to face an avalanche of New Deal labor legislation in the 1930s. In 1937 it reversed itself on minimum wages for women in *West Coast Hotel* v. *Parrish,* and in 1941 it finally unambiguously approved minimum wages for all workers producing goods intended for interstate commerce in *United States* v. *Darby,* thus upholding the constitutionality of the 1938 Fair Labor Standards Act.

The struggle over the ERA in the 1920s took place in a context in which women's organizations endorsed special legislation for women as part of a general reform effort to improve working conditions for women and men alike. The strategy worked with hours legislation, but it failed with wage legislation. In 1923 the National Woman's Party heralded the Supreme Court's decision in the Adkins case, allying itself with what the National Consumers' League considered reactionary political forces. The politics of gender and the politics of class were inextricably combined. At issue was not only what was best for women but what was best for American society as a whole. This clash of social visions was intensified in the late 1920s, when, reflecting the more conservative temper of the times, the Sheppard-Towner Act was allowed to die for lack of funding. The forces of progressive reform no longer could command legislative majorities at the state or federal level, but there was one thing they could and did continue to do long after the conditions that initially had generated their animosity had passed—oppose the Equal Rights

Amendment. Support for the amendment on the political left and within the ranks of organized labor came in the 1970s from a new generation that had not experienced "the women's war" of the 1920s.

NOTES

1. The best study of ERA opposition is J. Stanley Lemons's chapter "Feminists against Feminists" in his book *The Woman Citizen: Social Feminism in the 1920's* (Urbana: University of Illinois Press, 1973), pp. 181–208.

2. See J. Stanley Lemons, "The Sheppard-Towner Act: Progressivism in the 1920's," in ibid., pp. 153–80.

3. For biographical information on Florence Kelley, see Louise Wade on Kelley in *Notable American Women*, 3 vols, ed. Edward T. James, Janet Wilson James, and Paul S. Boyer (Cambridge: Harvard University Press, 1971).

4. Felix Frankfurter's "Foreword," in Josephine Goldmark, *Impatient Crusader: Florence Kelley's Life Story* (Urbana: University of Illinois Press, 1953).

5. See Stanley Kutler, ed., *The Supreme Court and the Constitution, Readings in American Constitutional History* (New York: W. W. Norton, 1977, 2d ed.), pp. 282–89.

6. Ibid., pp. 291–92.

7. Elizabeth Brandeis, "Labor Legislation," in John R. Commons, *History of Labor in the United States, 1896–1932*, 4 vols. (New York: Macmillan Co., 1935), vol. 3, p. 462. See also Anne Corinne Hill, "Protection of Women Workers and the Courts: A Legal History," *Feminist Studies* 5, no. 2 (Summer 1979): 247–73.

8. David Brody, *Steelworkers in America: The Nonunion Era* (Cambridge: Harvard University Press, 1960), pp. 271–73.

9. See Louis L. Athey, "The Consumer's Leagues and Social Reform, 1890–1923" (Ph.D. diss., University of Delaware, 1965), p. 221.

10. Ibid., p. 270.

11. Marianne Weber, *Max Weber: A Biography* (New York: Wiley and Sons 1975), p. 302.

12. Florence Kelley, "Need Our Working Women Despair?"*International Review* (Nov. 1882), pp. 517–26.

13. See Allen F. Davis, *Spearheads for Reform: The Social Settlements and the Progressive Movement, 1890–1914* (New York: Oxford University Press, 1967), p. 12 and passim.

14. For a list of eighteen women reform leaders in the social settle-

ment movement, see "Settlement House Leaders" in the "Classified Index," vol. 3 of *Notable American Women*.

15. See William O'Neill, *Everyone Was Brave: A History of Feminism in America* (New York: Quadrangle, 1969). This title was taken from a eulogy of Kelley at her memorial service, where Newton Baker said, "Everybody was brave from the moment she came into the room."

16. "The Woman's War," *New York Times*, Jan. 14, 1922. Clipping from Mary Van Kleek Collection, box 96, folder 1519, Sophia Smith Collection, Smith College.

17. See Lemons, "Feminists against Feminists," p. 190.

18. Ibid., pp. 181–208.

19. Ibid., pp. 187–189.

20. See Athey, "Consumer's Leagues," pp. 171–204; quote from Lemons, *The Woman Citizen*, p. 239.

Reasons for the Defeat
of the ERA

Joan Hoff-Wilson

Introduction

OPPOSITION TO THE ERA in the 1970s and 1980s should not be dismissed as simply the temporary product of a typically conservative postwar period. There was much more to the anti-ratificationist position than the fact that the country experienced such profound disillusionment—as a result of Vietnam, Watergate, and "stagflation"—that a national cultural and political backlash began in the mid-1970s, not equaled since the 1920s. In the course of 1973, domestic issues began to emerge as targets for this backlash, because the real questions of the war, national leadership, and the economy could not be simplistically understood or emotionally symbolized. The major objects of the negative national sublimation were busing, abortion, the ERA, and school prayer. Without a war to channel these frustrated emotions and without moral guidance from the White House, conservatives and fundamentalists launched a most successful grassroots campaign aimed at all things deemed unnatural and immoral. The profoundly irrational beliefs upon which this opposition, especially against the ERA, was based were nonnegotiable. Two value systems, two world views, two cultures suddenly impacted, but only one side knew it back in 1973.

As the following articles indicate, the anti-ratificationists viewed feminist individualism and the doctrine of equal rights as a threat or danger to the traditional differences between women and men and to the deferences accorded them by society because nature had so dictated. Those opposing the ERA wanted to be treated not as equal ungendered individuals but as a gendered class that enjoyed certain protections and differential treatment. They resented the fact that pro-ERA groups seemed determined to break the cultural solidarity of women's "rightful" place in society based upon their "special nature." They feared what would happen to them as mothers, wives, and workers if they were treated just like men. In the South and northern cities with large ghetto populations, this fear was exacerbated by racial prejudice. Thus the argument against *unisex* toilets really was one about *integrated* toilets in many areas of the country. Even when race was not an issue, washrooms restricted by sex represented "safe space" amid general male domination of the workplace.

Although such is not the conclusion reached by Jane DeHart-Mathews and Donald Mathews in the opening essay in this section, there is much in the most sophisticated version of the arguments of the anti-ratificationists which approaches the gender consciousness of the familial or relational feminists described by Karen Offen.* Unless the female cultural identity of the members of anti-ERA forces is recognized and distinguished from *both* the conservative era which encouraged it and the irrational public charges against the ERA which accompanied it, women who advocate complete equal rights with men will not succeed in obtaining passage of a future version of the ERA. Despite several major twentieth-century examples of relational feminists being co-opted by national and state objectives, such as in Nazi Germany, the Soviet Union, and China after their respective revolutions, and similar attempts at co-optation by the fundamentalists of the New Right in the United States today, its broad appeal cannot be ignored. NOW and other pro-ERA groups learned this historical lesson too late.

In addition to articles focusing on differing female values, culture, and rhetoric, others in this section focus on general strategies, particular tactics, and interpretation of poll data as ways to explain the defeat of the ERA in 1982. For example, both sides manipulated poll data to suit their own purposes. In the

---

*"Toward an Historical Definition of Feminism: The Contribution of France," Center for Research on Women working paper no. 22, Stanford University.

long run it probably did not make much difference that a Harris poll showed 63 percent of Americans in favor of the ERA in April 1982; or that in November 1983 a *New York Times* poll announced that only 48 percent of women believed that another attempt should be made to ratify the ERA; or that by March 1984 the ERA only placed sixth in a *Parade Magazine* poll purporting to rate the major concerns of U.S. women.

Passage of amendments to the federal Constitution does not depend on popular majorities or the lack of them. Mary Frances Berry* has argued convincingly that there are two major criteria that every addition to the federal Constitution must meet, because the Founding Fathers deliberately made the process very difficult by requiring a two-thirds vote of approval in Congress and three-fourths in the states. One is a preexisting consensus at the state level; the other is a sense of national necessity. These two "super majorities"—one at the congressional and one at the state level—can be prevented by a small, opposing minority. So national polls are of little value in estimating whether an amendment will pass. Clearly, proponents of the ERA could not generate real consensus in enough states, especially among women; and could not sustain the illusion that passage of the ERA was a matter of necessity for the country as a whole.

Consequently, as Berenice Carroll points out in her essay, the conclusion reached by *Ms.* in its January 1983 issue about why the ERA failed is simply wrong, whether judged by political, philosophical, legal, or linguistic standards. It is a testament to why the ERA failed that *Ms.* magazine could so misjudge why it failed. Both the strategies and tactics of NOW showed little historical knowledge either about the cultural importance of their opposition from the point of view of the average woman or about the lessons to be learned from passage of the Nineteenth Amendment by an earlier generation of U.S. women activists. Without a radical fringe group committing acts of civil disobe-

*Mary Frances Berry, *Why ERA Failed* (Bloomington: Indiana University Press, forthcoming).

dience in order to make ERA proponents appear more acceptable to mainstream Americans, and without consciously forged
alliances with conservative groups, especially after the war in
Vietnam ended, there was little hope for the quick passage so
many nationally prominent women expected after Congress approved the ERA in 1972.

In other words, what the ERA needed for ratification, among
many other things, was an Alice Paul and her followers, as well as
an Ellie Smeal and hers. Above all, the individualistic supporters of equal rights had to understand the collective fears of such
women for whom men represented a greater threat than could
possibly be offset by equal rights. Antiratificationists also viewed
women who wanted to act like men as the enemy—not the family
or traditional female attitudes and modes of behavior. When in
the 1970s individualistic and relational values clashed over the
ERA in a conservative postwar period reminiscent of the 1920s,
the anti-ratificationists were bound to win (just as they did in the
interwar years) unless the ratificationists demonstrated both a
sophisticated understanding of the opposition and a willingness
to compromise or ally with the least conservative segments of it.

Pro-ERA groups in the last two decades proved curiously
indifferent to their own history, especially when they began to
threaten anti-ERA politicians with gender-gap political threats.
Even though women share socialized attitudes, they never have
voted their views as a bloc because they are scattered throughout
the country at all socioeconomic levels. Therefore, the specter of
enough women voting together to change domestic or foreign
policies never materialized in the wake of the passage of the
Nineteenth Amendment—no more than it would have had the
Twenty-seventh been passed. To the degree suffrage and later
the ERA became a panacea among their respective supporters
and a pox on womanhood among their respective detractors,
both groups of women (and men) have operated on the false
assumption or illusion of a politically operative "gender gap."

One can only hope that perhaps someone or some group of

feminists will deal constructively with the deep-seated differences between individualistic and collective approaches to
reform that continue to exist among U.S. women here and
abroad. Until a way is found to bridge this gap between these
two very distinct brands of feminism, there is little hope for
ratification of the ERA in the near future or for gender-gap
politics to be effective in domestic or international arenas.

Jane Dehart-Mathews and Donald Mathews

The Cultural Politics of the ERA's Defeat

THE DEFEAT OF THE Equal Rights Amendment seemed virtually impossible in the spring of 1972. The Senate had joined the House of Representatives to submit the amendment to the states by an impressively lopsided vote of eighty-four to eight, suggesting that ratification would come as the natural product of the explosive egalitarianism of the 1960s. The exhilaration of con-

Reprinted by permission of Newspaper Enterprise Association.

frontation with authority and the excitement of what was thought to be rapid change had made the word *revolution* universal currency in the political marketplace. The civil rights revolution, the student revolution, and the cultural revolution telegraphed an impatience with the past and a hope for significant social change shared by some within government (the War on Poverty), as well as by those attacking its policies in Vietnam.

Young women, caught up in the cortex of protest, became self-conscious revolutionaries on their own behalf as they came to understand that personal experience separated them not only from the structure that they defied but also from male comrades whose limited understanding of sexual equality was epitomized by the draft resisters' slogan: "Girls Say Yes to Guys Who Say No." Joining with other women who differed substantially in style and ideology, these new feminists challenged a male-defined "reality." The mood of giddy optimism and dead seriousness was captured in a pamphlet published by the National Organization for Women entitled *Revolution: the time is NOW.* What was not fully appreciated in 1972 was that with revolutions come counterrevolutionaries. That these should have been women as well as men, and that they should have been as assertive as feminists, suggests something of the cultural ramifications of defeat.

Although there is no consensus to explain the ERA's defeat, there are several theories. For the victors, it resulted from an uprising of the people against irresponsible elites who had too long used government to meddle in private concerns. It was also a rejection of the feminist ideal of what women ought to be, an ideal that threatened to destroy the American family and sap the strength of a society already crippled by moral permissiveness and political weakness and indecision. Ratificationists had other explanations. Some—following the political axiom "If you can't defeat your enemies, attack your friends"—charged that Jimmy Carter had not done enough. Others claimed that banks and insurance companies, together with the Church of Jesus Christ of Latter Day Saints, spent great sums of money to defeat the amendment. Conservatives throughout the religious spectrum of Protestant-Catholic-Mormon-Jew had combined to resist subversion of patriarchal supremacy. Traditionalist male legislators had thwarted the public will. Men did it (which of course they did). It escaped no one's notice that archconservatives used the ratification fight to enlist otherwise elusive moderates in striking at the heart of liberalism—the commitment to equality. Finally, there was the manner in which anti-ERA women attacked ratification. It was a seemingly alarmist, shrill, hysterical, and perverse assault. Proponents believe that opponents lied and screamed the amendment to death.

In the process of a struggle over ratification, it became clear that, for conservatives as well as young radicals of the sixties, the personal had become political. But it was personal in a manner that did not seem authentic to pro-ERA activists. It did not arise from recognition of oppression and the conviction that sexism could be rooted out of laws, institutions, and customs. Nor did it come from an understanding of complex patterns of behavior and values that had socialized individuals in a male-defined culture. Rather, politicization of the personal came from women whose personal and familial experience made them wary of changes that would transform their way of life. Involved was defense against what was perceived as an attack upon them by feminists, resistance to placing their daughters and themselves in danger, and an assertion of self in a public drama. It is the meaning of this response that is the key to understanding opposition to the ERA and, by implication, the cultural context of its defeat.

Charges against the amendment had ranged over a broad spectrum to warn of "danger!" Ratification presumably would have meant drafting young mothers for combat. It would have meant the sexual integration of public restrooms, decriminalization of rape, legitimation of homosexuality, further entrenchment of abortion as a medical choice, increased opportunities for mischief from an interventionist federal bureaucracy, the loss by women of legal privileges, and the destruction of the American family. Responding to what they believed to be alarmist apocalypticism, ratificationists attempted to show how each objection was exaggerated, irrelevant, highly unlikely, or simply untrue. Taken altogether, the opposition seemed to be irrational and senseless or, at best, the political contrivance of a manipulative right.

Behind what proponents thought was senseless, however, there was and continues to be a pattern that lies within, behind, and beyond expressions of opposition—the elusive subjective experiences that anti-ERA women share with each other. These experiences flow from patterns of behavior and shared ways of talking about self and community. They provide coherence to one's life from the inner, subjective life of the individual, through common, everyday interaction with intimates, and beyond into the public life of work, social role, and frequently politics. Theorist Charles Taylor calls this coherence *intersubjective meanings*, the subjective experience of the social body, the meaning experienced in social practices that lies behind the flawed and incomplete expressions of it in public debate. Anti-ERA women no more doubted the authenticity of their position than did ratificationists, and for the same reason: subjective confirmation that they were right.

Public discourse is the window into the meaning that sustained anti-ratificationists. Take, for example, the draft. One of the most damaging charges was that the ERA would force young women into combat. Children carried signs reading "Please don't send my mommy to war!" When ratification was first debated, Americans had become accustomed to the images of terror and death flashing from their television screens. These images of danger overlay those of young men opposing the war, fleeing the draft, and deserting the army. Eventual withdrawal from Vietnam was part of this pattern of flight from masculine responsibility. The strength of America had been sapped. Somehow the women's movement was part of the degeneracy, the confusion of a society in which the authenticity of behavior and values based on the most basic and elementary fact of human life—sex—had been denied by misguided radicals. America was becoming a unisex society, said Phyllis Schlafly in disgust.

Within this mental context, women in the military meant a flight from responsibility by men and an anomalous intrusion by women into places where they had no reason to be. The facts that women were already in the military and that they had not been treated equitably there were irrelevant to opponents of the ERA. Women stepping out of female roles were women-who-want-to-be-men—anomalous persons who rejected the kind of life that nature (God and sex) had ordained. The implication of punishment for stepping outside of traditional roles was inherent in the dangers awaiting women in uniform. Thus, behind, under, and imminent in the image of women in combat was a cry of danger, the accusation of anomaly, and the implied threat of punishment.

The charge that the amendment would mandate the decriminalization of rape is the kind of alarmist mystification often characterizing right-wing rhetoric. While untrue, it does represent the sense of personal vulnerability that women felt when faced with the jumbled meanings of change associated with gender over the past fifteen years. For women who had so internalized traditional female roles that the very concepts of sexual oppression and emancipation seemed absurd, the temptation to reduce the ERA to an absurdity was irresistible. "If you *really* mean to enforce the law without reference to sex, you would have to wipe out all sex crimes. And, if you deny that, you do so because sex really does make a difference in how people should be treated, and this feminist blabbering about equality is just so much hokum." Beneath the accusation lay a sense of danger, the anomalous treatment of men and women as if "the same," and just punishment (rape) of women so foolish as to believe the sexes really were "the same."

This confusion of equality with sameness, and, therefore, with absurdity and danger, was also linked with impurity represented by anomalous men—homosexuals. Identification of gay liberation with women's liberation and the latter with the ERA was not a tortured reading of the contemporary feminist movement or of the sexual revolution, although it had nothing to do with legal equality guaranteed by the proposed Twenty-seventh Amendment. The words of the ERA, "on account of sex," were joined with "sexual preference" or homosexuality to evoke loathing, fear, and anger at the grotesque perversion of masculine responsibility represented by the women's movement. The linkage was a matter not so much of logic as of intuition. It is significant that although lesbians were identified in anti-feminist politics as women-who-want-to-be-men, they were not nearly so threatening as anti-feminists and homophiles, or men-who-refuse-to-be-men.

Charges that the ERA would entrench abortion, mandate sexual integration of public restrooms, and destroy the family seemed as irrelevant and mistaken to ratificationists as association of the amendment with homosexuality. Yet these indictments revealed the social-subjective reality underlying the opposition. The danger inherent in the cry that abortion was murder and that the ERA was the same as abortion is obvious. "Equality is the right of everyone," wrote a constituent to his senator, "but this ERA is a bad bill. No one, man or woman, has any right to murder babies."

Although ratificationists include pro-life as well as pro-choice partisans, identification of the ERA with abortion is pervasive and persistent. It is made not only for political reasons, but also because the conjunction represents feminists' presumed hatred of the biological function for which their sex had prepared them. The anomalous merges with the dangerous to allow condemnation of sexual irresponsibility—the trivialization of the sacred process by which human reproduction occurs. Women seeking abortion are women-who-refuse-to-be-mothers, which means women-who-refuse-to-be-women: anomalies. Implicit in the accusation that the availability of abortion allows "them" to "get off the hook" is an indignant sense of responsibility evaded and punishment denied.

As for the "potty issue," sexually integrated public restrooms became for pro-ERA activists a cross between comic relief and chronic despair. The image gathers in subconscious connections and anxieties which express more than the niceties implied in the term *ladies' lounge*. Restrooms had been integrated once before, that is, by race. And the word *integration* evokes memories of struggle over racial equality. Linking sexual equality with racial integration, ERA opponents parodied the latter with the "potty parable." Some troublemaker, denied access to the toilet of the opposite sex, would take the matter to the Supreme Court, which once again would order integrated facilities. It is not surprising that opponents of ratification should evoke roars of approval by pleading with state legislators not to "de-sexigrate" us.

Whether or not a serious statement, the idea of "integration" clearly captured the imagination of people who thought that the idea of equality—whether sexual or racial—was ridiculous. The ridicule seemed deserved, because equality was interpreted as sameness. As such, sexual equality implied a utopian, willful attempt to ignore cultural implications of a biological distinction. The sense of anomaly ran like a rich lode through the subterranean ethos of antifeminist argument. Objections to integrated toilets expressed in a different fashion the same diffuse sense of disbelief, frustration, and anxiety that was expressed in the emphatic "We don't want to be men." There was almost a religious intensity about the process, as if by calling attention to the anomalous, anti-feminists could cleanse themselves of the defilement of traditional roles perceived to have been heaped upon them by feminists (women-who-want-to-be-men).

The words *equality* and *integration* were also part of a generalized claim that the ERA would help to undermine the American family. Although vague and all-inclusive, the charge was meaningful for a variety of reasons. Many women understood the amendment to be a part of a feminist agenda to strip women of social roles defined by sex, which would mean that "mother" would be less an ideological or cultural concept than a biological one. The implied danger to the family was clear to nonfeminists; but it was also clear that the issue was not family life but rather its traditional form: father (head and provider), mother (nurturer and manager), and children (replicas of the older generation). The internal dynamics and quality of relationships independent of form were not so important to anti-ERA, pro-family forces as the ability of the father to stay out of the family, the mother to stay out of the job market, and children to stay out of public child-care facilities.

Changing the form of the family—or even acknowledging that there could be various forms—defied the orthodoxy of social roles defined by sex. The underlying sense beneath this accusation of anti-family engineering was represented in three images: loss of children, attack on homemakers, and the escape of husbands and fathers from financial responsibility. One of the most striking examples of losing one's children was their being "bused" from their homes into distant neighborhoods to achieve "racial balance." That represents to many parents their helplessness before a bureaucracy not directly responsible to them. Policies of the courts and the Department of Health, Education, and Welfare (now Health and Human Services) represented intrusions by the federal government into family life which would have been broadened by the ERA. If ratificationists argued that fears of such invasion were absurd, their opponents replied that no one had expected the absurdity of busing, either.

These and other responses to ratification suggest that the assault on the ERA was an assault on the ideal of equality. This displaced aggression was made possible by labeling feminism and sexual equality as absurd and dangerous. That was not a

sleight-of-hand trick by conservative politicians and busi-
nessmen, although there is no doubt that both groups fought the
amendment and that ultraright organizations such as the John
Birch Society and Eagle Forum exploited the issue to their own
advantage. It is also true that conservative religious leaders
played upon the fears of traditionalist women to defeat ratification. More significant, however, was resistance expressed in evo-
cative rhetoric that suggested a base of "intersubjective meanings" of womanhood and sex. Whether in New Jersey or New
York or Iowa or North Carolina, women repudiated state or
federal equal rights amendments because they had become the
symbol of feminism, an ideology profoundly alien to their experience of what it meant to be a woman. One did not have to be
manipulated by men or become gullible dupes of the patriarchy
in order to resist the claims of feminists to speak for women.
The process of socialization to which feminists were so sensitive
had been as subtle and indelible as theorists said it was, allowing
for an interpretation of personal experience that had been not
only meaningful but perhaps even rewarding for women who
believed that they were defending themselves in fighting the
ERA.

To understand this aspect of the ratification struggle as a
conflict over the meaning of womanhood is to place it within a
broad context of historical process that has yet to run its course.
The great numbers of Americans responsible for the steady drift
to the right since the presidential election of 1972 could see in
the issue of sexual equality—if successfully identified as absurd
and dangerous—a way to achieve political advantage. Anything
so engraved in us as experiences of what sex means could create
a broad base for conservative recruitment, especially in a postwar climate of conservatism. That was especially true after the
identification of sexual behavior with political liberation in the
sixties. When the personal became political for the "left," the
same thing was quite natural for the right. The result was the
fusion of the ERA with both feminism and liberalism.

That does not mean that in the long run either will have lost. Every historian knows that historical and cultural change is rarely abrupt. Changes within a generation are swift; the "inter-subjective meanings" passed from generation to generation result from a dialectic of which the defeat of the ERA is only one act among many stretching back in the past. The social base of feminism and protofeminism is much more secure now than in 1920. Although the experiences of women since that time have broadened considerably—the social base required for change—the failure of the ERA in 1982 was not as significant as the fact that a majority of Americans favored ratification. Given this achievement, the ideological concessions made to sexual equality by conservatives in a decade of debate may yet provide political capital to invest in a renewed effort to elaborate the insights of feminism and the genius of American egalitarianism and the weight of cultural baggage that sometimes prevents a swift de-pature from the past.

Janet K. Boles

The Equal Rights Amendment as a Non-Zero-Sum Game

NOW THAT LESTER THUROW has made the "zero-sum society" a part of the national lexicon, it is tempting to use that analogy to explain the politics of the Equal Rights Amendment. A zero-sum game is any game in which the losses exactly equal the winnings. For every winner there is a loser, and winners can exist only if losers exist. As a constitutional amendment, the ERA was not a compromisable issue in the way that pieces of legislation often are; it was either accepted or rejected in its entirety. This high-

"An Amendment to the U. S. Constitution the Only Way," cover of *Equal Rights: Official Weekly of the National Woman's Party,* July 28, 1923. Courtesy National Museum of American History, Smithsonian Institution.

stakes, zero-sum feature was at least partially responsible for the rancorous conflict which surrounded the issue for over a decade.[1]

On balance, however, the politics of the ERA are best understood as a non-zero-sum game. What opponents won during the ratification period was not directly translatable into corresponding losses for the amendment's supporters. The reverse is also true. Further, there were several ongoing ERA games, with multiple definitions of what constituted victory. To be specific, there were the ratification game, the public policy game, the public opinion game, the group-support game, the citizen mobilization game, and the issue-definition game.

The ratification game most nearly approximated the conditions of the zero-sum game. In the most narrow sense, victory for supporters was ratification; victory for opponents was non-ratification. However, even here the conditions for winning greatly differed. Ratification required the approval of thirty-eight state legislatures. If as many as thirty-seven had ratified the amendment by June 30, 1982, proponents still would have "lost" the ratification game. Opponents, by blocking ratification in as few as thirteen states, won.

Since 70 percent of the states approved the amendment, the ERA is correctly viewed as a genuine national policy trend. That so many state legislatures ratified the amendment is even more remarkable, since it is generally conceded that the side working for the adoption of any new policy is at a great disadvantage in American politics. The burden of proof rests with those seeking change; those who sought to block adoption of the ERA needed only to create a reasonable doubt in legislators' minds. The more controversial the issue and the higher the level of interest-group conflict, the greater the likelihood that the status quo will be retained.[2]

In view of the higher quantitative standards for ratification and the tendency toward inertia among decision makers once an issue becomes controversial, supporters should have been able to claim a moral victory. However, the perceived winners of the ratification game were clearly the opponents of the ERA.

The public policy game was an outgrowth of the ratification game. In fourteen states since 1970, voters approved a state ERA or a constitution containing such a provision. A general trend toward active state and national policy making and court decisions in the area of sex discrimination had also begun by 1972. A number of federal programs designed to end sex discrimination in employment and education were in effect. Furthermore, most states had passed one or more laws forbidding sex discrimination, often modeled upon the federal laws.

The courts, as well, were beginning to move against sex discrimination; the Supreme Court for the first time, in 1971, invalidated a state law discriminating against women. The procession of anti-sex discrimination laws and other legislation of interest to women accelerated after 1972, despite the difficulties the ERA encountered in several of the states. For example, legislation on equal credit and educational opportunities, rape, pregnancy disability, displaced homemakers, and flexible work hours was passed by Congress between 1973 and 1982. Although the court upheld several laws discriminating between men and women, a growing body of decisions striking down such laws emerged as well. The most contested policy for those playing the public policy game was the first federally funded National Women's Conference in American history, held in Houston, Texas in 1977.

For the most part, however, the public policy game was a one-person game, in that opponents of the ERA chose to concentrate on other games. Although ostensibly committed to equality for women *without* the ERA, opponents were not actively involved (on either side) in extending the legal rights of women through legislation or litigation. Victory here went to ERA supporters by default, robbing it of much impact. Ironically, the very success of amendment supporters in this game lent credence to the argument that sex discrimination could be eliminated through federal and state statutory revision and case-by-case litigation at various court levels.

In the public opinion game, both proponents and opponents attempted to convince legislators that they represented majority opinion on the issue and that their position was more consonant with existing social attitudes. ERA supporters considered it impressive that every poll taken from 1974 through 1982 indicated that a majority of the American public supported the proposed Equal Rights Amendment. The Harris Poll taken in April 1982 found that support for the ERA was at its highest level since 1976, with 63 percent of Americans in favor of it and 34 percent opposed.[3] Furthermore, polls indicated that at least a plurality of those groups commonly believed to form the core of opposition to the ERA—that is, people living in unratified states, housewives, political conservatives, and religious fundamentalists—actually supported the amendment.[4]

Opponents of the amendment commonly used polls which instead probed reactions to its potential impact. A 1971 Roper Poll, which was read into the *Congressional Record* by former senator Sam Ervin (D-NC), was widely quoted by the opposition.[5] It indicated that a majority of American women were hostile to the notion of men receiving alimony on the basis of need (68 percent) or of equal treatment for women in the military draft (77 percent). Again, public opinion shifted toward support of sex-neutral laws in these areas between 1971 and 1982. A 1980 Roper Poll found that only a bare majority (51 percent) of American women thought that men should not receive alimony under any circumstances.[6] Similarly, a 1981 Harris Poll found that only by 49 percent to 48 percent did a plurality of respondents, male and female, support the Supreme Court decision exempting all women from military registration.[7] These shifts may have been in response to earlier court decisions striking down sex-discriminatory alimony laws and then-President Carter's support for registration of both men and women.

These victories in the public policy game may have had a spillover effect on the public opinion game.

A final indicator of the clear victory by ERA supporters in this game was the dramatic increase in support for "most of the efforts to strengthen and change the status of women in society." When this question was first asked in 1970, a plurality of 42 percent favored these efforts, with 41 percent opposed. Support steadily grew into a substantial 67/29 percent majority in 1981.[8]

Supporters of the ERA could also claim victory in the group-support game. By the end of the campaign for state ratification, more than 450 organizations with a total membership of over fifty million were on record in support of the amendment. In an effort to achieve ratification before March 22, 1979, and also to demonstrate political clout, the National Organization for Women called for an economic boycott of unratified states in 1977. By March 1980, when the right of NOW to wage a boycott was upheld by the Eighth U.S. Circuit Court of Appeals, over 350 groups had voted to hold their conventions only in ratified states.[9] Many within this coalition of well-established and politically experienced organizations were also active participants in the congressional lobbying campaign which culminated in a thirty-nine-month extension of the deadline for ratification.

Formally in opposition to the ERA were a small number of previously existing national groups, such as the John Birch Society, the Daughters of the American Revolution, the American Conservative Union, and numerous ad hoc groups, primarily Phyllis Schlafly's STOP ERA. No organization in opposition previously had a national reputation for political effectiveness, and many, because of their far-right political orientations, had very negative public reputations.

Owing to certain perceived advantages accruing to proponents from this group-support game, it can be argued that ERA supporters were required to meet higher standards for victory in the citizen mobilization game. Proponent organizations, after all, were better known in the community and more reputable than the opposing ad hoc organizations; they had large memberships. In terms of economic resources, proponents could bank upon their national organizations and their broadly based memberships as continuing sources of funding. Opposition groups ostensibly depended solely on voluntary contributions from an ill-defined base of supporters.

The controversy served to politicize many citizens at the grassroots level who had no previous experience with political activism. The ERA also was an important device for recruiting new members into the contending groups. The rapid growth of the National Organization for Women was particularly notable. The organization's annual budget went from $700,000 to $8.5 million between 1977 and 1982, while its membership increased from 55,000 to 210,000.[10] And twice in the years 1979–82, close to 100,000 people gathered in Washington, and then in Chicago, to demonstrate their support for the ERA. Proponents, in short, were successful in mobilizing their constituency.

Those opposed to the ERA also shared this concern with demonstrating political effectiveness and attracting new members. It was felt that many of the amendment's opponents were interested in organizing women for participation in political conflicts in addition to that over the ERA. With the appearance of the so-called New Right in the mid-seventies, this interpretation assumed greater credence. The ERA emerged as one of the key issues uniting this new conservative political movement. Both legislators and the media correctly noticed that many women who had not previously been active in politics, either as individuals or as members of interest groups, were drawn into opposition ranks. This new social movement very quickly developed a strong organization, impressive funding, and a sophisticated electoral focus. Though the same was equally (or even more) true of the ERA's supporters, the perceived winner in the mobilization game was the opposition.

The success of the opposition in both the ratification and mobilization games was largely a result of its clear victory in the issue-definition game. ERA proponents attempted a public-education campaign only after the amendment encountered opposition in the state legislatures. The feeling was that if the ERA could be explained and grassroots enthusiasm for it engendered, legislators would then vote according to their constituents' wishes. The literature and other information provided by proponents on the subject dealt with the amendment's legal impact as interpreted in congressional documents and law review articles.

The opposition did not always restrict itself to the merits and demerits of the ERA itself. Instead, new and distinct issues, unrelated to the amendment, were injected into the debate. Some, such as abortion, were subjects on which the community was already divided; with the introduction of these new bases of emotional response, new participants and supporters were brought into the anti-ERA movement. Other issues, such as the sanctity of the home, were introduced and allowed for a response in only one direction.

In essence, opponents associated themselves with such valued institutions as the home, the family, motherhood, and religion, as well as with the strong national traditions of anti-Communism and all-male combat forces. Proponents had to rely on important but abstract values such as "equality" and "justice under the Law." Women, in particular, often felt that their life patterns were set unalterably, and the ERA would not be of much personal value. Potential benefits also seemed small in comparison with the possible upheavals envisioned by opponents. The extent to which ERA opponents succeeded in controlling the debate was reflected in opinion polls indicating that opposition to the ERA indeed centered around fears of increased competition between men and women, alteration of family structure, changed relationships between the sexes, and, to a lesser extent, the drafting of women.[11]

Regrettably, but inevitably, observers of American politics have focused upon the ratification game without noting how well or how fairly participants contested the other games surrounding the amendment. Nor have they considered the varying standards of performance required of the two sides. The outcome of the ERA struggle should not be an occasion for self-reproach by women's rights groups; nor should it be interpreted as a sign that the women's movement is dead or, at a minimum, without clout. The debate over the ERA served as the impetus for changing the course of public policy on the status of women in court decisions, federal and state laws, and bureaucratic procedures. It was accompanied by a virtual revolution in public opinion on the proper role and rights of women in society. Furthermore, the conflict mobilized women on both sides of the issue; it brought them together in coalitions and into politics. The political role of women changed; no longer can women be deemed "of aesthetic appeal rather than political import," as one scholar wrote in 1970.[12]

Notes

This essay is a revised version of remarks delivered at the Hutchins Center for the Study of Democratic Institutions, October 27, 1981.

1. For a more extensive discussion of the conflict over ERA ratification, see Janet K. Boles, *The Politics of the Equal Rights Amendment* (New York: Longman, 1979).

2. See James S. Coleman, *Community Conflict* (New York: Free Press, 1957), and Robert L. Crain et al., *The Politics of Community Conflict* (Indianapolis: Bobbs-Merrill, 1969).

3. Louis Harris, "Public Support for ERA Soars as Ratification Deadline Nears," *Harris Survey,* May 6, 1982, p. 1.

4. Mark R. Daniels et al., "The ERA Won—At Least in the Opinion Polls," *Political Science* 15 (Fall 1982): 578–84.

5. U.S., Congress, Senate, 8 February 1972, *Congressional Record* 118: 3072–73. This poll originally appeared in the Sunday supplement *Parade,* September 26, 1971.

6. *The 1980 Virginia Slims American Women's Opinion Poll: A Survey of Contemporary Attitudes* (New York: Roper Organization, 1980), p. 71.

7. Louis Harris, "Americans Favor Military Draft to Present Voluntary System," *Harris Survey,* September 24, 1981, p. 1.

8. Louis Harris, "Support Increasing for Strengthening Women's Status in Society," *Harris Survey,* August 17, 1981, p. 1.

9. "Organizations Supporting the Equal Rights Amendment," *National NOW Times,* May 13, 1980, pp. 14–15.

10. Barbara Salsini, "Wisconsin Fan Seeks Top NOW Post," *Milwaukee Journal,* September 2, 1982, p. 8.

11. See, for example, George Gallup, "Public Support for ERA Reaches New High," *Gallup Poll,* August 9, 1981, pp. 3–4; Joan Huber et al., "A Crucible of Opinion on Women's Status: ERA in Illinois," *Social Forces* 57 (December 1978): 549–65; Kent L. Tedin, "If the Equal Rights Amendment Becomes Law: Perceptions of Consequences among Female Activists and Masses" (unpublished paper, 1980 Annual Meeting of the Midwest Political Science Association).

12. Graham Wootten, *Interest-Groups* (Englewood Cliffs, N.J.: Prentice-Hall, 1970), p. 42.

Berenice Carroll

Direct Action and Constitutional Rights:
The case of the ERA

Assert, Demand, and Threaten -- with the use of $5 million in Federal funds given to the Commission on International Women's Year.
1

Boycott Convention Cities in Unratified States and cause financial harm to innocent people in hotels & restaurants.
2

Cut off Federal Funds and use White House lobbyists telephoning State Legislators, as well as other pressure out of Washington, D.C.
3

ON JUNE 3, 1982, a group of women calling themselves the Grassroots Group of Second-Class Citizens chained themselves to the railings before the Illinois Senate chamber in a demonstration favoring the Equal Rights Amendment. They remained

"Women's Lib Tactics to Browbeat States to Ratify ERA."
1. Reprinted by permission of United Feature Syndicate, Inc. 2. Courtesy Dick Hafer for the *Bowie Blade*. 3. Cartoonist Reg Manning, reprinted with permission of *The Arizona Republic*

· 63 ·

there for four days before being carried out of the capitol by the secretary of state's police at 4:20 A.M. on June 7. Members of the group then returned throughout the month of June to disrupt legislative sessions, to conduct sit-ins at the governor's office and on the floor of the House itself, and ultimately to write in blood the names of ERA opponents on the marble floors of the capitol building.[1] It was the most sustained series of militant actions in the history of the decade-long ERA ratification struggle and evoked intense reactions from both pro- and anti-ratificationists. Many proponents as well as opponents predicted that such "extremist" tactics would alienate people and turn legislators' votes away from the ERA.

In the end, there was little, if any, evidence that the vote count was significantly affected by the actions of the Grassroots Group. While one might conclude that that proves the essential inefficacy or irrelevancy of militant tactics, the campaign cannot be judged entirely—or even mainly—by its short-term impact on the legislative vote count. Direct action may appear to focus on short-term objectives and immediate, dramatic tactics, but in essence it is a long-term strategy for securing constitutional rights and social change.

In the January 1983 issue of *Ms.* magazine, Gloria Steinem and her coeditors argued that the ERA failed for three reasons: 1) too many people, both men and women, dislike women; 2) most of the majority expressing support in the polls remained, at best, complacently expectant instead of becoming politically insistent; and 3) the opposition was better organized.[2]

It is doubtful that this analysis can stand up under careful scrutiny. First, while the reality of widespread misogyny in this society is undeniable, the fact is that nationally the public, both men and women (whether or not they "dislike" women), overwhelmingly support the ERA. Moreover, when one examines closely the attitudes of women who opposed the ERA, as Jane DeHart-Mathews has done, it appears that it may be men, not women, whom they dislike.[3]

As to the second point, it is, of course, true, but it is not an explanation for the defeat of the ERA. The same can be said of the public on almost every political issue, and public nonengagement was equally evident—or, rather, more evident—when the ERA passed Congress and was ratified by thirty-five states.

As to the third point, it seems hardly demonstrable that the anti-ERA forces were "better organized" than the pro-ERA forces. The national and state ERA campaigns were superbly organized as political action and lobbying forces. As the Mathewses put it, the pro-ERA organizational style was marked by "leadership staffs, paid personnel, grass-roots action teams, organizational charts, computer printouts, poll data, telephone banks, and media spots . . . [with] formal structure, professional expertise, and rational argument based on skilled data collection and analysis."[4] The organizational methods and style of the anti-ERA forces were different, but that they were "better organized" is doubtful.

Why, then, did the pro-ratification campaign fail? Obviously, the answer must be a complex one. Other essays in this book address the broad cultural and political factors involved, particularly those relating to the substance and implications, or the imagined dangers, of the ERA, and to the right-wing coalition that opposed it.

Yet the question remains: Why did the legislatures of certain key states decline to ratify the ERA by narrow margins or by parliamentary chicanery, in defiance of the public majorities in favor of ratification in their states? First, in the face of organized opposition to the ERA after 1973, the predominantly male legislatures and executive offices of the nonratified states did not see the ERA as a priority sufficiently compelling to brook the opposition and risk its political costs. Second, the failure to make it a more compelling priority was not a failure of the "complacently expectant" public majority but was, at least in part, a failure of political policy and strategy (not organization), in particular the failure to incorporate tactics of civil disobedience and nonviolent direct action on a substantial scale.

Other essays in this book assess the role of militancy in the suffrage movement, and its association with Alice Paul, author of the ERA. Paul had returned from England in 1912 inspired by the militancy of the Women's Social and Political Union (W.S.P.U.), and had introduced some of its tactics to the U.S. suffrage movement. "Deeds Not Words" was their motto, as the militants picketed, disrupted meetings, chained themselves to gates and pillars, wrote slogans on sidewalks, defied police and courts, went to prison, and endured hunger strikes and forced feedings. On both sides of the ocean, the militants were a minority, and there were bitter internal struggles over the use of these tactics. In England, the W.S.P.U. moved ultimately to the destruction of property, smashing the windows of 10 Downing Street and elegant shops in London's West End, tearing up the turf of polo fields, disrupting mail and communication services, and even fire-bombing buildings.

These methods eventually split the Pankhursts from some of their most dedicated supporters, particularly Emmeline and Frederica Pethick-Lawrence, but Emmeline Pankhurst argued that the rulers of England understood nothing but property, and that by striking at them through property they would be brought to understand the necessity of granting women the vote. Yet throughout the struggle, the W.S.P.U. remained dedicated to nonviolence in the sense of noninjury to people. "The only recklessness the militant suffragists have shown about human life has been about their own lives and not about the lives of others," declared Emmeline Pankhurst, "and I say it here and now that it never has been and never will be the policy of the Women's Social and Political Union recklessly to endanger human life."[5]

Historians have differed greatly in exploring the role of militancy in the suffrage movement, as they have with regard to the role of militancy in every other movement for social change. The English suffragettes pioneered many of the methods of nonviolent direct action. Gandhi's first satyagraha campaign in South Africa in July 1907 followed by nearly two years the first imprisonment of Christabel Pankhurst and Annie Kenney for suffrage militancy in October 1905. Gandhi, while developing his own methods, was in correspondence with the suffragettes and observed their struggle directly during his first visit to England, in 1909.[6]

Since the first decade of the twentieth century, such methods have been adopted, developed, and extended in many contexts in this and other countries. Whether they have been "decisive" or "successful" (however that is measured), one reasonably may argue that they have played an essential part in the very complex processes at work in movements for social change. As Martin Luther King, Jr. wrote in his "Letter from a Birmingham Jail":

> You may well ask, "Why direct action? Why sit-ins, marches, etc.? Isn't negotiation a better path? . . . I have earnestly worked and preached against violent tension, but there is a type of constructive nonviolent tension that is necessary for growth. . . . Nonviolent direct action seeks to create such a crisis and establish such creative tension that a community that has constantly refused to negotiate is forced to confront the issue. It seeks so to dramatize the issue that it can no longer be ignored.

Militancy has been infrequent in the contemporary women's movement, but not entirely absent. The best-known examples have been associated not with the ERA but with struggles for reproductive rights and against misogynistic pornography.* In February 1969, women disrupted a New York state legislative

---

*Indeed one of the most obvious controversial examples of such an attack on liberal legalism can be found in the current debate over anti-pornography ordinances which several cities have attempted to pass or enforce. On this question, certain feminists not only are attempting to establish a new tort by arguing that pornography is a violation of women's civil rights, but they also are attempting to draft a legal definition of pornography which will pass muster under the First Amendment, in line with already existing exceptions to the basic free-speech guarantees associated with that amendment. How successful the anti-pornography feminists ultimately are, may well be an early indication of how effective or futile attempts will be to go beyond the defeat of the ERA into a new concept of justice for themselves and for society based less on individual and more on group rights.

hearing on abortion laws.[7] In the same month, a "nude-in" protest disrupted a *Playboy* magazine promotional appearance at Grinnell College. In April 1970, about thirty women occupied the executive office of Grove Press. In October 1977, Rochester Women against Violence against Women broke the display windows at a movie theater to destroy a poster advertising *Snuff,* spray-painted and chained the theater doors, and put glue in the locks.

> During our brief stay in jail [the Rochester women wrote later] many more women learned of *Snuff* [a movie purporting to show the actual murder and dismemberment of a young woman for the sexual stimulation of men]. The protests intensified. . . . We had acted in desperation, had not planned our arrest, and did not foresee the consequences of this action. The apathy that preceded our militant action disappeared after our arrest. Rather than alienating women, our dramatic and direct action inspired others to demonstrate against *Snuff.*[8]

Prior to 1980, militancy appears to have been absent (with one significant exception) or unknown in connection with the Equal Rights Amendment. Why Alice Paul did not pursue militancy in her decades-long advocacy of the ERA remains to be examined. Direct action did, in fact, play a key role in 1970 in gaining active consideration of the ERA in Congress. In February 1970, Wilma Scott Heide and a group of about twenty other members of the National Organization for Women disrupted hearings of the Senate Judiciary Committee on the eighteen-year-old vote to demand that hearings be scheduled on the ERA; before they left, Senator Birch Bayh (D-Ind.) had promised to schedule such hearings, which were held in May 1970.

If there were other incidents of direct action for the ERA in the decade of the 1970s, they seem to be lost to history. The disruption of the Senate Judiciary hearings in February 1970 was carried out by members of NOW, but not by NOW as an organization. NOW, which spearheaded the ERA ratification campaigns, never endorsed civil disobedience or other militant actions. Although NOW never adopted a formal policy against such forms of action, they did appear to have been informally discouraged. When this type of action began to reappear in 1980, it was not endorsed in the major ERA campaign organizations and was viewed with much doubt, if not hostility.

Nevertheless, incidents of direct action began to appear and spread around the country. On August 26, 1980, Women's Equality Day (the sixtieth anniversary of the suffrage amendment), twelve women chained themselves in front of the Republican National Committee headquarters in Washington, blocking the doors so that occupants were obliged to go in and out through the windows. On November 17, 1980, twenty-one women were arrested for chaining themselves to the gates of the Mormon temple in Bellevue, Washington. On Women's Equality Day in 1981, twenty women chained themselves to the White House fence, blocked the driveway, and were subsequently arrested for blocking the street. Women were arrested for climbing over the White House fence on February 15, 1982. On April 22, 1982, women trespassed on the governor's lawn in Chicago to protest Governor James Thompson's failure to give active support to the ERA, but they were not arrested.[9]

In the early spring of 1982, as the extended ratification deadline drew near with no encouraging signs of change in the unratified states, plans for direct action intensified, with a focus on Illinois. Illinois, the only northern industrialized state that still had not ratified, had a legislative majority favoring the ERA, but ratification was blocked by a three-fifths rule for constitutional amendments. While the Grassroots Group of Second-Class Citizens was formulating plans for civil disobedience in the capitol building, another group of women (some of whom had been involved in the earlier events mentioned above) began to plan for a different type of action: a fast, to begin in mid-May and continue until the ERA was ratified, or possibly until June 30, the ratification deadline.

A fast is not an act of civil disobedience, or a tactic of intervention or disruption. But a public fast is a highly confrontive, dramatic tactic with some of the characteristics of direct action. The seven fasters received widespread attention, locally, nationally, and worldwide. Their fast aroused tremendous sympathy among proponents of the ERA, despite much debate about its wisdom and effectiveness. The National Organization for Women, while not endorsing the fast as a tactic, agreed to support the fasters by providing accommodations and assistance. On the other hand, the fast aroused extreme hostility from opponents of the ERA, and exposed the unreliability of some alleged supporters. The fasters were vilified as "blackmailers," condemned for undertaking a "suicidal" course that would deprive their children of mothers, ridiculed as "dieters," and harassed by red-clad "antis" eating pizza and hotdogs in front of them during their daily vigils in the capitol. State Senator Forest Ethredge, an alleged supporter of the ERA, vowed to vote against the amendment and against any change in the three-fifths rule as long as the fast continued. Governor James Thompson saw fit to show his support for the ERA by telling the fasters when they arrived that the fast "would not change legislators' minds."

Some two weeks later, Thompson extended these supportive remarks to the tactics of the Grassroots Group of Second-Class Citizens: "All I'm saying is protesting, fasting and chaining isn't going to pass ERA [and] . . . is having counterproductive effects."[10] On June 8, Thompson went further and declared that he would not blame legislators for voting against the ERA because of the protest tactics.[11] Such remarks were surely not helpful. Moreover, they were fundamentally beside the point.

Governor Thompson was right in his prediction that fasting and chaining would not pass the ERA in June 1982, but direct action is not addressed primarily to an immediate change in legislative votes or government policies. Its short-term effect on legislators and officials is likely to be expressed in ridicule or outrage on the part of opponents and the indifferent, and in fear or revulsion on the part of uncertain allies. As Gandhi wrote in 1910:

> Of the many accomplishments that passive resisters have to possess, tenacity is by no means the least important. They may find their ranks becoming daily thinned under a hot fire. . . . They may be reviled by their own. . . . They may be misunderstood, and they must be content to labor under misrepresentation. . . . [They] must still stand their ground.[12]

Direct action must be understood as a process which requires time to gather impact. It is a process of both action and reaction, a process of exposing and dramatizing repressed levels of conflict, with the ultimate objective of changing the balance of forces. The process does not end with the dramatic actions themselves, or even with the immediate reactions of authorities, press, and public. It continues with debate and dialogue on those actions and reactions, with analysis and evaluation, with similar actions repeated elsewhere. If the process fails to gain momentum, it will be limited in impact but may resurface, even decades later, with other persona. Direct action seizes the imagination and consciousness of participants and observers with experiences not readily expunged.

Crystal Eastman wrote of this process as it operated in the suffrage movement:

> Indifference is harder to fight than hostility, and there is nothing that kills an agitation like having everybody admit that it is fundamentally right. . . . As I look back over the seven-year struggle I sometimes suspect that many bold strategies were employed more to revive the followers than to confound the enemy. . . .
> Organizing the women voters of the suffrage States to defeat democratic candidates, picketing the White House, the hunger strike, burning the President's war speeches—each of these policies was begun under a storm of protest from within and without the movement. Yet each proved in the end good political strategy

and at the same time had an enormous re-enlivening influence on the suffrage movement. Those who stood by suffered so from the almost universal criticism that they gained the power and faith of crusaders. And the more conservative suffragists who opposed these policies were stimulated to more and more effective action along their own lines from a sense of rivalry. And so the movement grew and grew from the mighty dissension in its ranks.[13]

Eastman focuses here on the effects of direct action on the movement itself, effects of rallying followers and challenging critics within the movement. The process of direct action also has effects upon a wider public and upon those in positions of authority. To both these groups it makes highly visible and urgent a conflict or a demand that has been obscured by silence, indifference, timidity, conformity, apathy, or despair, and impresses on them the depth of commitment to the cause on the part of its adherents. At the same time, it imposes certain costs upon those authorities whose actions or policies are directly confronted by the demonstrators. It exposes them to public scrutiny, and requires them to confront, on a face-to-face basis, those who are seeking to hold them accountable by a public, bodily witness. In addition, it imposes upon them tangible costs in money, time, energy, personnel, resources, reputation, and psychological stress. These costs may have the initial effect of engendering anger and hostile responses, but in the long run, such costs must be weighed in the balance by lawmakers when they determine their priorities.

That these effects were not negligible in the campaign conducted by the Grassroots Group of Second-Class Citizens in Springfield, Illinois in June 1982 is attested by many sources, from press and television coverage to the arguments of the secretary of state's attorneys in court hearings and briefs. One of the clearest testimonies appeared in an article in *Illinois Issues* by Diane Ross of the capitol press corps. Ross arrived at a rather unsympathetic conclusion about the "chain gang," as the press generally called the group, but acknowledged its dramatic impact upon a legislature in which the ERA "had never claimed the priority of either party":

> It was the chain gang—not the fasters—that electrified the atmosphere in June at the Statehouse. Attitudes toward the protestors shifted from tolerance to tension; nerves were frayed, blood pressures went up. Then legislators literally lost their tempers. It was the sit-in around the speaker's podium—not the splattering of blood on the floors in front of the doors to the House, Senate and Governor's Office—that made legislators mad as hell and determined not to take it anymore. It was the disruption of the proceedings of government—not economics, not politics—that in a single day turned this least dramatic of sessions into the most dramatic. No one had ever dared to confront legislators on their own turf. No one had ever been allowed to walk onto the floor of the House, march down the aisle, sit down in front of the speaker's podium. No one, no one from the outside that is, had ever caused the House to adjourn in chaos—and gotten away with it. The disruption stunned the House.[14]

Historically, direct action has stood in a dual relationship to constitutional rights. On the one hand, it often has taken the form of extraconstitutional means to achieve goals of social justice. On the other hand, it frequently has been used to secure constitutional rights unlawfully denied, as in civil rights struggles, or not yet recognized, as in the suffrage movement.[15] Direct action is not always civil disobedience, and the line between demonstrations which are unlawful and those which are constitutionally protected forms of freedom of speech and assembly may fall in a grey area of interpretation where governmental authorities and the Supreme Court have disagreed (for example, *Cox v. Louisiana*, 1965; *National Socialists v. Skokie*, 1977). Even where direct action crosses over into civil disobedience, however, it is essentially nonviolent in character. Nonviolent demonstrations may call down violence on the demonstrators, and sometimes they may respond spontaneously with violence.[16] Direct action may also involve destruction of property, as noted above. But in intent and method, both direct action and civil disobedience are unarmed and nonviolent in the sense of rejecting injury to people as an acceptable means. Campaigns of armed and systematic violence may be called revolution, insurrection, guerrilla warfare, or terrorism, but not direct action. It is, in fact, its unarmed, nonviolent character that distinguishes direct action as a militant approach to seeking social change or constitutional rights.

That the campaign of direct action carried out in Springfield in June 1982 did not win ratification of the ERA was no surprise. The use of these tactics in the preceding years had been too isolated, cut off from endorsement and support by the main organizations conducting the ratification campaign, and beset by inexperience and doubt. Under those conditions, there was no time for the long-term impact of direct action to develop. But members of the Grassroots Group of Second-Class Citizens believed that it was necessary to launch this strategy before the ERA went down, as an expression of the anger and commitment of women conscious of their second-class citizenship, and as a signal for the future.

Whether feminists will take up civil disobedience as a major part of the general stretegy of the women's movement today remains to be seen. The fact that Sonia Johnson won 40 percent of the vote for the NOW presidency in October 1982 on a platform advocating more confrontive tactics is highly suggestive, but the form and rallying points of future militancy are still unclear. Perhaps it was too early to adopt such a strategy before the defeat of the ERA, but perhaps that defeat—temporary as it is—will prove to have given the impetus to a renewed, and more militant, mobilization of energies to secure constitutional equality for all people, regardless of gender.

NOTES

1. A photograph of the Grassroots Group of Second-Class Citizens (unnamed) appeared in the January 1983 issue of *Life* (*Year in Review* issue). Berenice Carroll was a member of the group and participated in some, but not all, of the group's actions; for consistency and to avoid claiming undue credit, she refers to the group in the third person.

2. *Ms.*, January 1983, p. 37.

3. Jane DeHart-Mathews, "The ERA and the Myth of Female Solidarity" (American Historical Association paper, December 29, 1983).

4. DeHart Mathews, "ERA and the Myth," pp. 4–5.

5. Albert Hall Speech, October 17, 1912.

6. *Suffragettes*, a term first used by opponents to demean the suffragists, was later adopted by the W.S.P.U. as a badge of honor and was the title of their journal (after their split with the Pethick-Lawrences) in the years 1912–14; in the United States, it remained a term of opprobrium for the suffragists.

7. Robin Morgan, *Sisterhood Is Powerful* (New York: Random House, 1970), p. 278.

8. Laura Lederer, ed., *Take Back the Night* (New York: William Morrow, 1980), pp. 263, 268, 272, 282.

9. Personal communications from participants.

10. Bloomington *Pentagraph*, June 5, 1982, p. A7.

11. *WCIA News*, June 8, 1982.

12. Louis Fisher, ed., *The Essential Gandhi* (New York: Random House, 1963), p. 92.

13. Blanche Cook, ed., *Crystal Eastman on Women and Revolution* (New York: Oxford University Press, 1978), pp. 65–66.

14. Diane Ross, *Illinois Issues*, August 1982.

15. April Carter, *Direct Action and Liberal Democracy* (New York: Harper and Row, 1973).

16. See Carter, *Direct Action*.

Edith Mayo and Jerry K. Frye

The ERA: Postmortem of a Failure in Political Communication

THE RHETORIC OF A SOCIAL and political movement is crucially important to its success in persuading the public to adopt its goals. Rhetoric reveals the self-images and ideology of the movement, the images which the movement wishes to convey to the public, the nature of the existing grievances to be remedied, and positive visions of a future society that results from adoption of the proposed changes. The audience must identify with the rhetoric in order to be persuaded. If persuasive appeals do not achieve mass public acceptance, the movement fails.

This review of the rhetoric of supporters and opponents of the ERA uses arguments characteristic of the period and examines their continuity during the sixty-year debate. The rhetoric of each side was an accurate expression of the two sides' divergent views of the nature of women and women's roles in society. An examination of the shifts and modifications in persuasive tactics will provide a clearer understanding of the ERA's failure to be ratified.

Rhetorical strategies employed throughout the debate included scare tactics, which raised questions of constitutional chaos and painted mental pictures of dire consequences resulting from the ERA; righteous rhetoric, which used Judeo-Christian traditions of women as subordinate and subservient to men as a part of God's divine plan, employed Biblical injunctions to fortify arguments, and invoked God as the ultimate male authority figure; use of the superior wisdom of male authority figures to buttress arguments; certitude against probability, which capitalized on the fears and lack of legal knowledge of the general public about the ERA; defense of the status quo, which was presented as most advantageous to women (a variant was the theme of women's "privileges" which would be abrogated by the ERA, Schlafly's "We don't want to stoop to equality"); *ad hominem* arguments, which used personal attacks and name calling and demeaned ERA proponents as negative, unattractive, repulsive, deviant, and threatening; ridicule as social control, which made ERA proponents appear ridiculous and resulted in laughter and dismissal of the ERA; trivialization of women's legislative grievances; and diversionary and red-herring tactics, which employed such arguments as the implication that the ERA was the wrong method, substituted counter legislative measures and amendment riders, and raised the issues of "potty politics," homosexuality, and abortion.

The Equal Rights Amendment was introduced in Congress in 1923 by the National Woman's Party (NWP), which realized that the vote did not create legal equality for women. The NWP and the mainstream suffragists, represented by the National American Woman Suffrage Association (NAWSA), held very different views of "women's nature" and the roles of women in society. The NWP advocated total equality for women as a matter of right and justice, and its rhetoric accurately expressed that view. During the 1920s, ERA arguments crystalized on both sides, centering on the "special nature" of women and their need for protective legislation.[1]

Originally intended to safeguard women from exploitation in industry, protective legislation was viewed by the NWP as a form of reverse discrimination that hindered women's opportunities. NWP spokeswoman Doris Stevens declared, "Protective legislation, no matter how benevolent in motive, unless applied to both sexes amounts to actual penalization."[2] The NWP asserted that if women were recognized and treated as equals, they could protect themselves: "Modern woman does not want the support granted to a dependent; she wants to and should be an equal partner."[3]

Opposing the Woman's Party, on both the ERA and the concept of women's nature and roles, was an impressive group of "social feminists," including the League of Women Voters (successor to the NAWSA), the National Consumers' League, the Women's Trade Union League, and the Women's Bureau of the Department of Labor, veterans of the suffrage movement and the drive for protective labor legislation. Rhetoric against the ERA stressed that women were more susceptible to disease, were less suited to heavy manual labor, and needed shorter working hours. It was argued that women's health had to be safeguarded for the propagation of the race. Heavy emphasis was placed on biological differences between men and women; on woman's "special" psychosexual nature, her different mission in life, and her frailty; and on fears of exploitation of women's "weaker" status both physically and economically. Esther Dunshee of the LWV said, "Protective legislation recognizes a biological difference between men and women and takes into account that conservation of our womanhood means the preservation of the race."[4] Supporters of protective legislation such as Florence Kelley of the National Consumers' League stated: "The cry Equality, Equality, where Nature has created inequality, is as stupid and as deadly as the cry Peace, Peace where there is no Peace."[5]

Throughout the ERA's history, opponents used the "superior wisdom" of male authority figures to make telling points. In 1924, Felix Frankfurter, then a professor at the Harvard Law School, established a pattern of interweaving arguments that pervaded the rhetoric throughout the ERA's history:

> The legal position of woman cannot be stated in a single simple formula. . . . The law must have regard for woman . . . as an individual, as a wage-earner, as a wife, as a mother, as a citizen [constitutional chaos will result from ERA]. Only those who are ignorant of the nature of the law . . . or indifferent to woman's industrial life will have the naivete or the recklessness to sum up woman's whole position in a meaningless and mischievous phrase about "equal rights" [ridicule as social control]. . . . Law must accommodate itself to the immutable differences of nature. For some purposes . . . the law must treat them as men and women [legal argument from women's physical differences]. . . . The Woman's Party would do away with all differences which arise from the stern fact that "male and female created He them." The Woman's Party cannot amend nature [righteous rhetoric and invocation of God as ultimate male authority figure].[6]

In the 1930s, rhetoric on both sides remained basically unchanged. Arguments based on women's biological/physical differences and on protective legislation were accentuated by the economics of the Depression. Frequently, righteous rhetoric, women's physical differences, and protective legislation were combined by opponents during the 1930s. Senator William Borah (R-ID) declared: "I do not believe women have the right to work in dangerous places on the same level as men. It seems to me we are trying to do what God has failed to do—make them equal when they are not equal. It is not a question of superiority, it is a question of physical differences."[7]

Changes in ERA rhetoric were brought about by the passage

of the Fair Labor Standards Act in 1938, which allowed some protective labor legislation for men. Equally important was the climate favoring equality in the Second World War and the impetus given by the adoption of the equal rights provision of the United Nations Charter. Arguments on protective legislation were rendered particularly ineffective, because protective laws for women were nullified during the war by the need to employ women in industry. Alice Paul, leader of the NWP, expressed the supporters' challenge of equality in wartime: "When the United States is engaged in a war with the avowed purpose of establishing freedom and equality for the whole world, [it] should hasten to set its house in order by granting freedom and equality to its own women [rights and justice argument]."[8]

With protective rhetoric diminished in the 1940s, ERA opponents emphasized strong anti-feminist arguments: women should not have legal equality because they were different biologically and socially; women were not equal but indeed "specially privileged."[9] While "women are and of right ought to be equal with men, [they] can never be on a level with men . . . just because nature made them different and society has so long placed them in a position different from men."[10]

The Committee to Defeat the Unequal Rights Amendment argued that the lack of equality was a positive good. Ten distinguished women (among them Carrie Chapman Catt, Eleanor Roosevelt, Frances Perkins, Mary Anderson, Mary McLeod Bethune, and Rose Schneiderman) predicted that the ERA would bring the loss of women's "privileges" such as Social Security provisions for mothers and wives, and veterans' and workmen's compensation allowances for wives and widows.[11] Senator Abe Murdock (D-UT) stated: "To protect the women in performing their functions the various states . . . have seen fit to pass laws which discriminate against men and are in favor of women."[12]

In a clever strategy that plagued public perceptions of the ERA thereafter, opponents incorporated anti-feminist ideology into an Equal Status Bill (1947), making it appear that the ERA would require the sexes to be "identical in nature" rather than "equal under law." Opponents were thus assured that the physical, biological, and social differences would still be taken into account legally.

NWP spokeswoman Alma Lutz summarized the 1940s proponents' arguments of justice in a democracy: "Human rights and fundamental freedoms are above physical structure and biological function . . . they belong to every human being, and need no safeguards before they are offered to women."[13]

The social feminists' view (embodied in the Equal Status Bill) was summarized by Frances Perkins, the influential former Secretary of Labor:

> The unique biological function of women and their responsibilities as homemakers and mothers; . . . women's different physical structure and greater susceptibility to fatigue and exhaustion; the dual responsibility of women who are homemakers as well as wage earners; the need to safeguard the health and welfare of women workers for the sake of developing a healthy, happy, and competent national population [make protective legislation imperative].[14]

Ironically, during the Second World War there was little significant rhetoric about fears that the ERA would make women subject to the draft equally with men. It was also ironic that in the decade of the 1940s, when the climate favored equality, internecine feuding and legal suits within the NWP itself sapped supporters' strength at a critical time.

A peacetime postwar economy made it necessary for women employed in wartime occupations to return to the home. Strident arguments were made by government and the media to return women to their "proper sphere," and emphasis on home and family was all-pervasive. Protective legislation was resumed, paving the way for rhetoric on protection.

Opponents developed a major new diversionary tactic in the

1950s: amending the amendment. In this "decade of the riders," the Senate passed the ERA with a rider proposed by Carl Hayden (D-AZ) in 1950, 1953, and 1960, thwarting the intent of the ERA by allowing "exemptions" from equal treatment and protective legislation. Senator Estes Kefauver's (D-IN) Biological Status Bill and other amendment riders were a denial of equality cloaked in protective, paternalistic concern and chivalric male rhetoric.

Emanuel Celler (D-NY), chair of the House Judiciary Committee, refused to hold hearings on the ERA for twenty-three years! He prevented the amendment from leaving his committee for consideration on the floor between 1948 and 1971. Celler used an argumentative tactic employed since the 1920s: the assertion that the ERA was the wrong method.

> We cannot deny that discrimination against women is present. . . .
> It is not defense of these laws that makes for opposition to the
> present amendment. It is the method that is decried. Using the
> Constitution for a broom with which to sweep away indis-
> criminately the good with the bad is neither sound law nor sane
> behavior. [Note the use of the domestic metaphor and ridicule as
> social control.][15]

Political and social changes in the 1960s created renewed support for the ERA. The civil rights movement, with its tactical militancy and demands for minority rights, nurtured the growth of feminism. Title VII of the Civil Rights Act of 1964 voided protective legislation based on gender, eliminating the major rationale for opposing the ERA since its introduction. Many labor and women's groups traditionally opposed to the ERA reversed their positions and supported the amendment.

The formation of NOW and the rebirth of the women's movement in the late 1960s and early 1970s brought renewed fervor to the fight for the ERA. Before congressional passage, however, the opposition assumed many of its old forms. Leadership in thwarting the impact of the ERA through riders was taken up by

Senator Sam Ervin, Jr. (D-NC), a master of righteous rhetoric who joined traditional anti-ERA tactics with this unique rhetorical hyperbole:

> We find in the Book of Genesis . . . "God created man in His own image. . . . Male and female created He them." . . . The law should make such distinctions as are reasonably necessary for the protection of women and the existence and development of the race. When He created them God made physiological and functional differences between men and women. . . . Some wise people even profess the belief that there may be psychological differences.
>
> The physiological and functional differences . . . empower men to beget and women to bear children. . . . From time whereof the memory of mankind runneth not to the contrary, custom and law have imposed upon men the primary responsibility for providing habitation and a livelihood . . . to enable their wives to nurture, care, and train their children.[16]

Ervin cited male legal authorities to support his anti-ERA claims (inappropriate method and constitutional chaos). Constitutional expert Paul Freund of the Harvard Law School stated:

> I am in wholehearted sympathy with the efforts to remove . . . vestigial laws that work an injustice to women. . . . However, not every legal differentiation between boys and girls, men and women, husbands and wives, is of this obnoxious character, and to compress . . . [them] into one tight little formula is to invite confusion, anomaly, and dismay.[17]

Opponents found the draft issue a particularly strong argument, which they exploited skillfully. Opponents used gut-level rhetoric and concrete imagery to conjure up fear about the specter of women in combat, which goes against the entire cultural concept of women as life-givers and nurturers of children. Senator Ervin's rhetoric epitomized the visual imagery of opponents:

The amendment [would] . . . convert Annapolis, West Point, and other service academies into coeducational war colleges. . . . If [it] is added to the Constitution substantial numbers of women will be enrolled in the Armed Forces to serve in combat. . . . These women will suffer the loss of their privacy and sometimes become pregnant and bear illegitimate children; the amendment will prohibit the discharge from the armed services of any single woman for pregnancy or child bearing, no matter how often she becomes pregnant or how many bastards she bears. I am satisfied that the veterans who waded in the icy waters in trenches until their feet bled during the First World War . . . who endured the heat of North Africa and the Anzio beachhead . . . during the Second World War, and the veterans who fought in the mountains of Korea and the steaming swamps of . . . Vietnam are implacably opposed to having . . . [the ERA] subject American girls to similar experiences. And I am sure that the fathers and mothers of the daughters of America agree with them.[18]

Some of the feminist daughters, however, disagreed, as this refutation from the George Washington University Women's Liberation Group indicates:

We, as draft-age women, deplore the proposition . . . that if we demand equality of rights, we deserve the punishment of the draft. . . . The draft is now being used to intimidate women in their efforts to gain . . . rights. Senators who pose the threat of conscription are obscuring the issue of our equality. . . . We again attest to our equality and demand equal application of the Selective Service Law. . . . No, we do not want to die in Viet Nam. But neither do we want to be told that our place is one of servitude to the male power structure, that our only role in life should be as mothers and housewives. . . . Ervin's brand of protection . . . perpetrates the insidious discrimination based on sex that now exists in every area of our lives [and] that implies an elitist sexist attitude of the superior capability and intelligence of men.[19]

Such strident feminist rhetoric was typical of the women's movement's failure to construct persuasive answers to the draft for a general, nonfeminist public.

"Potty Politics," the fear that the ERA would nullify laws requiring separate restrooms and bath facilities for men and women, was introduced to plague the amendment. Senator Ervin stated that "[supporters] contend that the amendment will not nullify laws requiring segregated rest rooms for the sexes. . . . The amendment contains no [such] exception or limitation, and is absolute in its terms."[20]

Once ratification was underway, opposition crystalized in earnest. Phyllis Schlafly's STOP ERA and right-wing coalitions mounted an extremely effective campaign employing classic rhetorical tactics. As primary spokeswoman for the opponents, Schlafly was visually pleasing, clever, articulate (if not accurate), and poised, and could not be charged with male chauvinism. Her rhetoric was unerringly on target.

Schlafly's name calling was devastating to ERA supporters. She characterized the ERA's advocates as "liberationists" and "a bunch of bitter women seeking a constitutional cure for their personal problems." She characterized ERA support tracts as "sharp tongued, high-pitched whining complaints of unmarried women."[21] Her readers were urged to view photographs of an ERA rally and "see for yourself the unkempt, the lesbians, the radicals, the socialists."[22] ERA supporters were repeatedly labeled "militant," "arrogant," "noisy," "aggressive," "hysterical," and "bitter."[23] Her scare tactics expressed the fears of traditional women. The ERA would "positively, absolutely, and without the slightest shadow of a doubt make women subject to the draft. . . . Women will be sent into combat and on to warships with men. . . ." Traditional housewives were fearful of Schlafly's assertion that the ERA "will make a wife equally responsible to provide a home for her family . . . and 50 percent of the financial support." She successfully convinced many that the ERA was "a total assault on the family, marriage, and children."[24]

Schlafly sternly warned that the ERA would rob women of their present "privileged status" (the group's name was an acro-

nym: STOP ERA = Stop Taking Our Privileges). Schlafly declared:

> Of all the classes of people who ever lived, the American woman is
> the most privileged. We have the most rights and rewards, and the
> fewest duties. . . . Why should we lower ourselves to "Equal
> Rights" when we already have the status of "special privilege?"[25]

Schlafly's rhetoric and approach were summed up succinctly by
the slogan "You can't fool Mother Nature."

The central theme of the sixty-year debate between supporters and opponents of the ERA was their differing concepts of
women's nature. In the earlier years, opposition rhetoric focused
on women's weaker physical nature and the need for protective
labor legislation. Once that issue was effectively countered, the
emphasis shifted from economic factors and women's weaker
physical strength to sexual/socio/psychological arguments concerning the destruction of the traditional home, women's roles,
femininity, and the "nature of womanhood." Throughout the
ERA's history, there was an implicit assumption that *men* constituted the norm and that women and their life situations were
abnormal or deviant.

The primary failure of the ERA's supporters throughout was
their inability to devise effective persuasive appeals that made a
clear distinction in the public mind between "political and legal
equality" and "sexual sameness." This confusion gave ERA opponents a lethal advantage which they skillfully exploited.

Schlafly and her STOP ERA coalition did not invent anti-
feminist rhetoric; they inherited it as a coherent body of successful opposition rhetoric fully developed, articulated, and employed over many decades by social feminists and congressional
opponents. Schlafly needed only to rework the arguments into
the current jargon of the New Right and the Moral Majority. In
a subtle philosophical change, Schlafly altered the debate from
the "true nature of womanhood" to a debate over the "nature of
true womanhood" (Schlafly's "positive woman," whose life re-

volved around husband, home, and children) into a debate come full circle since the mid-nineteenth century.

The ERA was not separated from the rhetoric of the modern women's movement. Persuasive appeals did not sufficiently differentiate between the ERA and the highly controversial issues of homosexuality and abortion. Much of the public perceived the rhetorical and nonverbal images used by segments of the women's movement as essentially strident and negative (radical, loud-mouthed, militant, stringy-haired, anti-male, braless "libbers"). These were outrageous and offensive images, because they did not fit accepted cultural concepts of women. They occurred at the same historical moment as the outset of the debate on ERA ratification. The negative image of "libbers" and their perceived attack on the family and traditional social and personal relationships was transferred to the ERA and firmly and irrevocably fixed in the public mind. While iconoclasm was necessary to liberate women from traditionally confining stereotypes of the past, "women's lib" rhetoric made an excellent target of attack for opponents of STOP ERA. Supporters failed to perfect affirmative rhetoric that fit prevailing cultural concepts of women or to project concrete, positive visions of how the ERA would benefit women.

The failure to ratify was additionally a failure of access to national network channels of mass-media communication. Modern mass communication research strategies were not fully used because of lack of money and political and communication expertise. The persuasive techniques of the earlier women's movement were adapted to the media dissemination of that day; those of the modern women's movement and the ERA campaign generally were not. Before the final year of ratification, the modern women's movement continued to use essentially the same techniques, perfected over long years of experience in women's rights issues (lobbying, lectures, leaflets, pamphlets, journals, buttons), but generally failed to make the transition to modern campaign techniques.

Prior to the 1970s, argumentation about the ERA was waged primarily within the closed circles of congressional hearings and lobbyists, or as an exercise in preaching to the converted within the forums and publications of the two factions of the women's movement itself. This pattern continued within the groups of the modern women's movement. Even the early ratification campaign was waged successfully within state legislatures, where proponents' rhetoric for passage was expressed primarily in terms to which legislators or those in the women's movement could relate. The techniques perfected in those arenas were inappropriate for mass-media communication appeals necessary after 1973, when the stalled ratification effort forced a change in the audience. The movement perfected few new techniques, slogans, or positive visual images appealing to a general, non-feminist audience. It failed to sell the ERA to nonfeminist women. Pitted against STOP ERA scare tactics and their realistic, graphic imagery and gut-level rhetoric, much of the public had difficulty in relating to ERA supporters' use of abstract, intellectualized, and legalistic images and appeals to "rights" and "justice." The public knew little of the previous debate, and NOW's "media blitz" of 1982 came too late to educate them about the ERA.

ERA supporters should begin planning strategy *now* for the next serious effort to pass the Equal Rights Amendment. (The ERA already has been reintroduced in Congress.) Supporters should take opponents' arguments seriously (no matter how ridiculous they may appear, they reflect a vast reservoir of genuine uncertainty and discomfort) and be prepared to beat them at their own game. Proponents also can recognize that the same rhetoric cannot be used to sell the ERA to a mass audience as was used for consciousness raising within the women's movement. Effective, persuasive appeals must be developed based on realistic, positive images of women. Changes brought about by the women's movement could be presented in affirmative, non-threatening rhetoric describing the benefits to both sexes.

Cogent responses could be developed for issues of the draft, personal privacy, abortion, and homosexuality. "It's About Time" that the ERA was promoted with current media techniques. With careful strategy and renewed commitment, indeed, "The Battle's Not Over."

NOTES

1. NWP was viewed as radical in the 1920s. Its postsuffrage membership declined from 50,000 to 8,000 between 1920–23. See Hazel Greenberg and Anita Miller, eds., *The Equal Rights Amendment: A Bibliographic Study*, 1976, p. xii.

2. *Forum* 72 (August 1924): 151.

3. Lady Willie Forbus, "The Lucretia Mott Amendment," *Equal Rights*, April 26, 1924.

4. *Woman Citizen*, March 8, 1924, p. 19.

5. Florence Kelley, "The New Woman's Party," *Survey* 45 (March 5, 1921): 827.

6. *Congressional Record*, March 28, 1972, pp. 10450–56.

7. *Hearings*, February 7, 1938, pp. 51–52.

8. *Congressional Digest* 20 (April 1943): 107.

9. See Loretta J. Blahna, "The Rhetoric of the Equal Rights Amendment" (Ph.D. diss., University of Kansas, 1973), p. 60.

10. "Equal Rights," *Woman's Home Companion*, April 1939, p. 2.

11. Letter to the Senate, S.J. Res. 61, July 18, 1946, *Congressional Record* 42, p. 9401.

12. *Congressional Record*, July 18, 1946, p. 9225.

13. "Only One Choice," *Independent Woman*, July 1947, p. 199.

14. House of Representatives, *Hearings on ERA*, 1945.

15. *Congressional Record*, March 7, 1950, p. A2054.

16. *Congressional Record*, March 28, 1972, pp. 10450–56.

17. *Congressional Record*, September 10, 1970, p. 31132.

18. *Congressional Record*, March 28, 1972, pp. 10450–56.

19. *Congressional Record*, March 2, 1972, p. 6765.

20. *Congressional Record*, March 28, 1972, pp. 10450–56.

21. Lisa C. Wohl, "The Sweetheart of the Silent Majority," *Ms.*, March 1974, p. 56.

22. *Schlafly Report* 5, no. 7 (February 1972).

23. *Schlafly Report* 9, no. 11 (June 1976).

24. Wohl, "Sweetheart," p. 57.

25. *Schlafly Report* 5, no. 7 (February 1972).

Significance of the Defeat of the ERA

Joan Hoff-Wilson

Introduction

IT WILL BE SOME TIME before all of the legal ramifications of the defeat of the Equal Rights Amendment will be known. Part of the difficulty in assessing its legal importance or lack thereof arises from what appears to be a confusing array of Supreme Court decisions since 1971 that deal with gender. Even the most cursory examination of these decisions reflects a mixed constitutional bag for women. In contrast, Congress and the executive branch of government, until the Reagan administration, have provided more consistent leadership than the Supreme Court on women's rights over the last twenty years.

Beginning in the 1960s, a series of congressional acts, executive orders, and guidelines issued by government agencies created to enforce affirmative action marked a quantum leap in the legal status of U.S. women. The breakthrough began with the Equal Pay Act in 1963, Title VII of the 1964 Civil Rights Act, and two executive orders in 1965 and 1967 (nos. 11246 and 11375) prohibiting certain kinds of discrimination by federal contractors. It continued in Congress with Title IX of the 1972 Educational Amendments and a 1978 amendment to Title VII requiring employers to provide employee benefits for pregnancy-related disabilities.

In 1981 Congress passed legislation allowing state courts to divide military pensions equally when long-term marriages end in divorce, and in 1984 it approved legislation facilitating the enforcement of child-support payments and the collection of pension payments for women. All of these actions have greatly aided women in their battle against sex discrimination in the work place, in educational institutions, and in their roles as wives and mothers, and finally laid to rest the controversy over protective legislation and equal rights.

Even before the courts in the early 1970s began to interpret liberally Title VII of the 1964 Civil Rights Act, protection of women versus equal rights for women had become a false issue; yet it persisted in dividing women reformers in the 1940s, 1950s, and 1960s. Only one woman could have ended this destructive struggle following the Second World War—Eleanor Roosevelt. However, she not only led the Democratic women who supported New Deal reforms but also had long been in the protective legislation camp. Thus, both her politics and her brand of relational feminism kept her from ever using her enormous power and influence to heal the wounds created by the bitter debates between the protectionists and equal rightists in the interwar years or to work publicly for passage of the ERA between 1945 and her death in 1962.

Without a single leader to unite them, women continued to fight each other until the Second Women's Movement emerged in the late 1960s, when actions take by Congress (some of which overturned Supreme Court decisions) aided both the healing process and the cause of women's legal equality with men. Supportive Supreme Court decisions did not begin to appear in the 1970s. Elizabeth F. Defeis points out in her essay that as of 1976 the Justices established a middle level scrutiny test for sex discrimination cases. The problem with this approach is the same as for any other standard of review; namely, that the test can be manipulated by the Supreme Court to achieve the results it wants. Both Nancy S. Erickson* and Wendy Williams**have commented extensively on how the Craig standard has been variously applied through manipulation of the "dissimilarly situated" theory.

*"Historical Background of 'Protective' Labor Legislation: *Muller* v. *Oregon*," in D. Kelly Weisberg, ed., *Women and the Law: A Social Historical Perspective* (Cambridge: Schenkman Publishing Co., 1982).
**"The Equality Crisis," *Indiana Law Journal* 56, no. 3 (1981):175-80, 200.

Ratification of the ERA would not automatically have remedied this problem stemming from idiosyncratic juridical interpretation. In 1984, for example, the Supreme Court ordered the U.S. Jaycees to admit women and said that law firms may not discriminate on the basis of sex which lawyers to promote as partners. At the same time in *Grove City College* v. *Bell,* it gutted Title IX by deciding that individual units of educational institutions could discriminate and not endanger the federal aid received by other units, saying receipt of Basic Educational Opportunity Grants by some students did not require institutionwide coverage under Title IX. At the end of 1984, Congress failed to override this decision with provisions in a Civil Rights Restoration Act.

Despite an inconsistent record, the courts have undoubtedly improved the legal status of women in the last twenty years without an Equal Rights Amendment. Ratification of the ERA would have contributed significantly to this ongoing process. It would not have immediately produced uniform treatment of women under the law or guaranteed consistently favorable court decisions.

In the wake of the ERA's defeat, we are disposed to forget that this amendment, like the Fourteenth before it and all previous civil rights acts, was designed not to change values but to modify behavior of mainstream citizens by changing the constitutional status of a particular group. The ERA's purpose was (and is) to provide equality of opportunity through the Constitution and legal system for those women who want to realize full personal and professional expectations within mainstream America.

Had the ERA been ratified, it would have been absolutely noncoercive when it came to individual lifestyles, because its enforcement powers were directed only against state and federal agencies or public officials, not against private citizens. It also would not automatically have changed public policy based on remaining sexist assumptions about women. Nonetheless, the passage of the ERA in 1982 gradually would have promoted legal uniformity in the treatment of females in state and federal statutes in a way that no previous acts of Congress, executive orders, or Supreme Court decisions could.

Ultimately, the ERA may be more important in defeat than in victory, as a symbol of how far women still have to go to obtain true constitutional equality with men in American society. Its defeat has forced advocates of civil rights for women to seek creative legislative and judicial solutions in their continuing struggle for full and equal legal status with men. It already has resulted in a greater questioning of public policy that continues to inconvenience women, such as the lack of comparable pay scales and the incompatibility of the working hours of banks, post offices, and other private or public institutions, such as schools, with the typical nine-to-five shifts of working mothers.

The success of the Nineteenth Amendment lulled into complacency many of those in the First Women's Movement. Perhaps the failure of the Twenty-seventh will inspire those in the Second Women's Movement to continue to strive not only for legal rights but also for public-policy changes which will positively affect the everyday lives of women and begin to restructure society to meet their needs.

Just as first suffrage and then protective legislation emerged as avant garde reforms, they ultimately were replaced with other issues, such as equal pay for equal work and finally the Equal Rights Amendment. These issues, in turn, are now being replaced by ideas about comparable worth and questions about whether women should simply settle for obtaining equal rights that are still basically determined by individualistic male standards. Perhaps before the end of this century, women in the United States will reunite behind a more relational, female-oriented approach to improving their status and society, but as of the mid-1980s, there is every indication that the equal-rights approach remains dominant here, if not in the rest of the Western world.

Elizabeth F. Defeis

The Legal Impact of the Equal Rights Amendment

OPPONENTS OF THE PROPOSED Equal Rights Amendment have often claimed that the ERA is unnecessary—that sufficient safeguards against gender discrimination presently exist in the Constitution of the United States. The combined effect of the Nineteenth and the Fourteenth amendments, it is argued, affords

"Don't Just Stand There—Open the Door for Us" Courtesy Don Hesse and the *St. Louis Globe-Democrat*.

both women and men adequate protection against any state or federal sex-based illegal actions. The legal history and tradition of these two amendments, as well as recent decisions, will be explored to determine their legal impact.

The Nineteenth Amendment, adopted in 1920, granted women the right to vote in all elections. It was silent, however, on any concurring rights: for example, the right of women to run for elective office or otherwise to participate in the governing process. Consequently, the states were free to interpret the scope of the amendment for themselves, and the only consistent interpretation of the Nineteenth Amendment was the extension of suffrage to women. Thus, it did not necessarily include the ancillary right to run for and hold public office or the right to appointive office without regard to gender qualifications. Despite some early decisions to the contrary, elective and appointive offices have been opened to women through judicial decision, legislation, or a combination of the two and clearly, under the Fourteenth Amendment, as currently interpreted, a woman's right to hold public office could not be restricted because of gender.

The Fourteenth Amendment, however, although initially construed narrowly, now has a much broader impact and speaks to the issue of equality. The Equal Protection Clause of the amendment states that "no State shall . . . deny to any person within its jurisdiction the equal protection of the laws." In recent years, the Equal Protection Clause has been invoked to strike down laws which discriminate against traditionally disfavored groups such as racial minorities, aliens, and illegitimates. Building on these cases, those opposed to the ERA argue that the Fourteenth Amendment could be used to strike down infringements upon many rights on the basis of gender.

The Supreme Court has developed three distinct levels of scrutiny to apply to a claim of discrimination under the Fourteenth Amendment: strict, middle, and minimum. Most classifications—such as health requirements or safety regulations—

are afforded mere minimum scrutiny by the court. The court will inquire into the legislative permissibility of the law: does the state have a rational basis for the law; does the classification established by the state bear a reasonable relation to the objective of the law so that the law treats similar persons similarly? Since the burden of proof under this test is easy for a state to meet, the great majority of these state laws and/or actions have been held not to violate the Equal Protection Clause.

At the opposite end of the spectrum are classifications which are subjected to "strict scrutiny" by the court. This highest level of judicial scrutiny is warranted either when the legislative classification is inherently "suspect" (such as race or creed) or when the legislation affects a "fundamental right" (such as voting, travel and interstate movement, and, more recently, privacy). In these instances, it is not enough that the state show a rational basis; rather, the state must show a compelling interest for the classification or infringement upon fundamental rights. For all practical purposes, this compelling state interest is never found to be present by the court, and, thus, laws which invoke strict judicial scrutiny are deemed by scholars to be "fatal in fact."

The Supreme Court has vacillated in its decisions as to the appropriate level of scrutiny to employ when examining gender-based classifications. Prior to 1971, the court used minimum scrutiny to determine the constitutionality of gender-based state laws. In *Goesaret v. Cleary,* the Supreme Court upheld a Michigan statute which provided that only daughters or wives of male owners could tend bar. Denying that the statute violated the Equal Protection Clause, Justice Felix Frankfurter lightly dismissed the contention that the statute was motivated by the desire to restrict employment opportunities in bartending to males:

> Since the line they [legislators] have drawn is not *without a basis in reason,* we cannot give ear to the suggestion that the real impulse behind this legislation was an unchivalrous desire of male bartenders to try to monopolize the calling. [emphasis added]

As late as 1961, the Supreme Court in *Hoyt* v. *Florida* unanimously upheld a Florida statute which automatically exempted women from jury duty unless they expressed an affirmative desire to serve.

However, in 1971 the Supreme Court questioned the automatic acceptance of legislation that classified on the basis of gender. In *Reed* v. *Reed,* a female petitioner challenged an Idaho statute which provided that when heirs were equally entitled to administer a decedent's estate, males would be given preference over females. Significantly, the court never applied "minimum scrutiny analysis" or "strict scrutiny analysis," but instead applied a somewhat ambiguous standard. Speaking for the court, Chief Justice Warren Burger wrote:

> The Equal Protection Clause . . . does, however, deny to states the power to legislate that different treatment be accorded to persons placed by a statute into different classes on the basis of criteria wholly unrelated to the objective of that statute. A classification must be reasonable, not arbitrary, and must rest upon some ground of difference having a fair and substantial relation to the objective of the legislation, so that all persons similarly circumstanced shall be treated alike.

The court acknowledged that the state's objective of reducing the workload of probate courts by eliminating one class of contestants was not without merit. It concluded, however, that giving a mandatory preference to members of one sex over members of the other, merely for administrative convenience, is to make the very kinds of arbitrary legislative choice forbidden by the Equal Protection Clause of the Fourteenth Amendment.

The broadest statement of the court concerning equality of the sexes occurred in 1973 in the case of *Frontiero* v. *Richardson.* A federal statute allowed an armed-forces serviceman to claim his wife as a dependent, regardless of whether she in fact was dependent upon him for any part of her support. A servicewoman, on the other hand, could not claim her husband as a

dependent (and, thus, obtain increased allowances) unless he
was dependent upon her for over one-half of his support. It was
argued that this statute unreasonably discriminated on the basis
of sex in violation of the Due Process Clause of the Fifth Amendment. Justice William Brennan, announcing the decision of the
court, declared that sex (like race) should be a "suspect classification" and that the court should, correspondingly, utilize a strict
scrutiny test when examining legislation which discriminated on
the basis of gender:

> Moreover, since sex, like race and national origin, is an immutable
> characteristic determined solely by the accident of birth . . . and
> what differentiates sex from such non-suspect statutes as intel-
> ligence or physical disability, and aligns it with the recognized
> suspect criteria, is that the sex characteristic frequently bears no
> relation to ability to perform or contribute to society. As a result,
> statutory distinctions between the sexes often have the effect of
> invidiously relegating the entire class of females to inferior legal
> status without regard to the actual capabilities of its individual
> members.

Applying the strict scrutiny analysis mandated by suspect classification, Justice Brennan determined that no "compelling interest" existed for the disparate treatment, and accordingly, found
the federal statutes unconstitutional. Significantly, five of the
justices, although concluding that the statute was unconstitutional, did not join the court's opinion in holding sex a suspect
classification, reducing Brennan's position to a mere plurality of
justices.

   In the years following the *Frontiero* decision, the Supreme
Court has effectively retreated from its position of adding gender to the list of suspect classifications. However, in 1976 the
court developed a "middle tier," or special tier of scrutiny, to be
applied to gender-based classifications. In *Craig* v. *Boren*, the
court held that gender classifications should be analyzed using a
two-prong test: 1) the classification must serve important govern-

mental objectives; and 2) it must be substantially related to the achievement of those objectives.

Craig v. *Boren* considered the constitutionality of an Oklahoma statute which prohibited the sale of 3.2 percent beer to males under the age of twenty-one and to females under the age of eighteen. It was argued that the gender-based disparity "denied to males 18–20 the equal protection of the laws in violation of the Fourteenth Amendment." Justice Brennan, writing for the court, reiterated that a state's interest of "mere administrative convenience" was not sufficient to justify a gender-based classification. Rather, for any classification based upon gender to pass constitutional muster under this middle-level scrutiny, the state must first prove that the classification serves an "important governmental objective." However, what constitutes an important governmental objective is not outlined by the court but, rather, must be determined on a case-by-case basis. The second component of the middle-tier scrutiny test, namely, "the classification must be substantially related to the achievement of the important governmental objective," is also without articulated standards.

In the area of economic rights, the court has invalidated legislation which burdened either males or females. In most cases, such laws are viewed as reinforcing gender-based stereotypes. In areas involving other than economic rights, the court has resolved the cases with ambiguity and has not yet adequately developed standards to determine whether such gender-based classifications are constitutional.

Recent cases in the 1980s illustrate the ambiguity inherent in this middle-tier scrutiny. For example, in 1981 the court, in *Michael M.* v. *Superior Court,* examined the constitutionality of California's statutory rape law. The law provided that intercourse with a young woman under the age of sixteen years was illegal. No similar law existed to cover young men of the same age. Utilizing the *Craig* test, Justice Rehnquist concluded that the California rape law served the important governmental objective of protecting against teenage pregnancies, despite the fact that the rationale for statutory rape laws historically has been to protect young women legally deemed to lack the capacity to consent to intercourse. Thus, since only teenage women potentially could become pregnant, as opposed to teenage men, the court held that the classification was, indeed, substantially related to this governmental objective. Thus, the Supreme Court upheld the state's statutory rape law as constitutionally permitted within the "middle-tier" scrutiny analysis.

In the same manner, the court also upheld in 1981 the provision of the Military Services Act requiring the registration of males but not females for military service. In *Rostker* v. *Goldberg*, Justice Rehnquist, again writing the majority opinion, emphasized the great deference that the court grants to Congress in the area of national defense and noted that women were forbidden by federal statute from serving in any combat positions. Applying the *Craig* test, Justice Rehnquist determined that the important governmental objective involved was the drafting and preparation of "combat troops." Since only men could legally serve in combat, gender classification "fit" the government objective and was constitutional. In these two 1981 cases, the Supreme Court chose to define the important governmental objective in a manner which would "protect" women rather than afford them equality.

Another illustration of this middle-tier scrutiny is the court's opinion in the 1982 case *Mississippi University for Women* v. *Hogan*, which involved the validity of a single-sex, state-supported nursing school. The exclusion of males was invalidated by a sharply divided court. The court held that since women were not underrepresented in the field of nursing, the governmental objective advanced of compensating females for past discrimination was not furthered. The court specifically declined to address the question of whether single-sex schools in areas other than nursing violate the Fourteenth Amendment.

Although the public has focused attention upon the ERA only

since the early 1970s, argument and debate over the amendment are not recent phenomena. In fact, the ERA, in some form, had been introduced in Congress every year between 1923 and 1970; Congress considered it seriously in 1946, 1950, 1953, and 1970, and once again in 1983 the Senate Subcommittee on the Constitution began hearings on the proposed amendment.

While experts disagree on many of the details of the strategy for adoption of the ERA, there is consensus on one general point: the fears generated about the ERA were a significant factor in its failure to obtain ratification. Perhaps the most vocal concern that was advanced by the opponents of the ERA is that the ERA will prohibit privacy based upon sex. Such fears are grounded upon a misconception concerning the law of privacy.

Though the text of the Constitution does not explicitly recognize a "fundamental right of privacy," in *Griswald* v. *Connecticut* the Supreme Court held that such a right implicitly exists. Further, the court has held this right "fundamental" and has placed it, judicially, in a highly protected position along with the right to interstate travel and the right to vote.

The ERA must of necessity be construed together with this concomitant right of privacy. As early as 1964, the courts held that individuals have a constitutional right of privacy in police searches of their clothing and their person. Similarly, while such separate facilities as restrooms or sleeping quarters would not be invalid under the ERA, it would require that they be equal in quality, convenience, and otherwise.

Besides a concern with the effect the passage of the ERA would have on the "all-male" military draft, many Americans are also worried about its impact on the financial arrangements of marriage. They fear that the ERA would prohibit women from receiving alimony after a divorce or would require all women to provide 50 percent of the financial obligation for their husbands and children. However, the ERA will require the alimony obligation and the family financial obligation to fall upon only the spouse who can economically assume it; if both spouses can assume it, then each will assume it in proportion to her or his resources. The Supreme Court has already adopted this attitude in the case of *Orr* v. *Orr*. Economic reality at the present time dictates that the husband, who is usually the major breadwinner in the two-parent family, provide the bulk of alimony and family support. However, in cases where the wife is the primary bread-winner, she will shoulder the majority of the financial obligation.

Passage of the Equal Rights Amendment would clearly have an impact on existing law. By prohibiting governmental action that discriminates on the basis of gender, the court would require a strict scrutiny test to determine whether a gender classification is constitutional. As has already been noted, in the area of racial classification, a strict scrutiny test is, in fact, fatal to the classification.

While passage of the ERA would add clarity to an ambiguous area of the law, it should not be viewed, at this time, as the exclusive avenue available for securing the goal of legal equality. Rather, there is extensive federal as well as state legislation mandating gender equality in such areas as employment and education. Implementation of such existing laws should be vigorously pursued. One might also consider American ratification of international covenants and treaties which prohibit gender discrimination as a goal to be achieved in this decade. The ratification of treaties as a means of obtaining equality for women in the United States appears to have been largely neglected. A number of international agreements in effect at present and ratified by many countries (but not the United States) provide for political, social, and economic rights for women.

These conventions warrant the attention of those who seek to eliminate gender-based discrimination in the United States, as well as those who believe that the United States should play a more active role in the promotion of human rights internationally. The achievement of legal equality for women in the United States should not be limited to a single legal strategy; rather, a concerted effort should be made to explore every method which could implement the promise of equality now found in the Constitution.

Elizabeth Pleck

Failed Strategies; Renewed Hope

As OTHER ESSAYS in this collection have noted, the Equal Rights Amendment was first proposed in 1923 by the National Woman's Party, the militant wing of the suffrage movement. The purpose of the ERA was to overturn the hundreds of gender-based legal statutes through the passage of a single constitutional amendment. For decades, interest in the amendment languished, and was then reawakened with the rebirth of the women's movement

"Now Is the Time for All Good Men to Come to the Aid of NOW!" Courtesy L. D. Warren for the *Cincinnatti Enquirer.*

in the 1960s. In 1972, the amendment passed both houses of Congress and was sent to the states for ratification. A decade later, however, the ERA went down to defeat when only thirty-five state legislatures ratified it—three short of the required thirty-eight.

Soon after the defeat, Eleanor Smeal, then president of the National Organization for Women, claimed that the ERA had been betrayed by the Republican party (which refused to endorse the amendment in its platform in 1980) and by a dozen male legislators in key states. Feminists other than Smeal began to wonder whether the defeat of the ERA reflected deep-lying prejudice against women. Some have blamed the proponents of the ERA for using the wrong tactics; others have credited its opponents with superior tactics and organization. In their chapter in this book, Jane DeHart-Mathews and Donald Mathews argue that opponents of the ERA were astute in their ability to associate the amendment with feminism and liberalism. The purpose of history is not to assign blame but to understand the reasons for what has happened. There were not one but several reasons for the defeat of the ERA. It lost because it failed to summon enough votes in state legislatures, owing to the culture of the times, the organization of the proponents and opponents, and the nature of the amendment itself.

The most difficult thing to explain is how an amendment which was so popular with the American people could have been defeated. In the midst of a national conservative tide, popular support for the ERA was very strong.[1] The last opinion poll before its defeat, taken in July 1981, showed that 63 percent of the public favored ratification. Public support for the ERA even shot up five points between 1981 and 1982.[2] Much of the increase in public approval came from the growth in support of the ERA among American women, who had previously been less likely than men to approve of the amendment. Contrary to the popular stereotype that full-time homemakers opposed the amendment, public opinion polls showed that they were as likely to favor the ERA as women earning wages. Most religious fundamentalists and political conservatives favored the ERA, and even in unratified states majority sentiment supported the amendment.[3] The ERA not only enjoyed broad public support but also had the backing of national leaders and influential national organizations. Every American president since Harry Truman, with one notable exception, has supported the amendment. Major national organizations from the American Bar Association to the Girl Scouts had gone on record in favor of it. If the ERA was so popular, why was it defeated? How did an extremely popular idea so quickly become transformed into a lost cause?

Some of the seeds of defeat were apparent even in the time of the ERA's greatest victory, when in 1972 it passed the House by a margin of 354 to 23 and carried the Senate by 84 to 8. The National Organization for Women, in concert with other liberal organizations, had centered most of its efforts on the passage of federal civil rights legislation and the enforcement of those laws at the national level. Once the ERA finally had been moved from committee onto the floor of Congress to be voted upon, NOW and other liberal organizations launched a massive letter-writing campaign. They also had the distinct advantage of riding the crest of interest and enthusiasm for women's rights. The Congress that passed the ERA in 1972 generated more women's rights legislation than all previous congressional sessions combined.

After this resounding victory, women's organizations assumed that there would be no need for a state ratification campaign. Lopsided early victories for the ERA in small and northern industrial states eager to jump on the bandwagon of equal rights for women appeared to confirm the belief that victory was at hand. The ERA Ratification Council, a coalition of thirty proponent groups, had been formed shortly after congressional passage of the amendment to work for ratification in the states. But as late as December 1973, the council had no staff, no printed materials for distribution, and only a small budget. The council appointed a strategy committee, which, sensing its own ineffectiveness, met once and voted to disband.[4]

There was no ratification strategy at all in 1972. Most of the innovative tactics employed to achieve passage of the ERA— fund-raising walkathons, fastings, national television advertising, and an economic boycott of unratified states—were not devised until after 1977, when it was certain that the ERA was in trouble. But if one looks more closely at the structure of the National Organization for Women in 1972, it is clear that it was not equipped for an extensive campaign in the states. The ERA then was only one of several issues of concern to NOW. The organization had no more more than 15,000 members and a relatively small budget. Even if NOW had possessed the resources to involve itself in state politics, it would have had difficulty making coalitions with conservative or moderate state legislators because of its liberal political stance. But in 1972, proponents of the ERA were anticipating an easy and quick victory. The opposition of organized labor, concerned about the nullification of protective labor legislation for women, had been neutralized. Only the Ku Klux Klan, the John Birch Society, and a group calling itself Happiness for Housewives appeared to be opposed.

Had no organized opposition to the ERA developed, the amendment would have passed in 1973 or 1974.[5] Had the ERA gone to the states a couple of years before 1972, when the national mood was still ebullient, its chances of passage would have increased sharply. But opposition did develop, and, with hindsight, the proponents appear ill-advised not to have been prepared for it. The formation of STOP ERA by Phyllis Schlafly, a Barry Goldwater conservative, caught women's organizations unaware. Only after Schlafly's STOP ERA began to score victories in 1973 was a strategy for ratification developed, a national fund-raising campaign begun, and a national headquarters with a paid staff established.

Schlafly did not begin to organize STOP ERA until after the amendment had gone to the states. But 1973 was an extremely propitious time to begin marshaling opposition to the ERA. It was, after all, the year in which the Supreme Court ruled in *Roe* v. *Wade* (1971) in favor of liberalized abortion statutes. Soon after the court issued its ruling, groups began to form to overturn it. In 1973, there was no connection between the opponents of liberalized abortion and the opponents of the ERA. But there soon would be, as these single-issue groups began to coalesce into a more general opposition to the sexual, cultural, and political changes of the 1960s, an opposition which called itself the New Right.

Phyllis Schlafly was one of the propagandists from the Old Right who was able to make the transition to become a leader of the New Right. The Old Right's dominant issue—opposition to Communism—had lost much of its appeal by the 1960s, but no issue or set of issues had replaced it. Aware of this problem, the right sought issues of concern to a large part of the population. In 1971, Schlafly, who had written a highly popular campaign tract in favor of Barry Goldwater's candidacy for president, was concerned about the missile gap with the Russians, and was crusading against détente and the SALT treaty. A conservative friend of hers had tried to interest her in opposing the ERA in Congress, but she had not been interested. When asked to debate the amendment that year, she told a friend, "I'm not interested in ERA. How about a debate on national defense?"[6]

But when Schlafly began to read about the ERA, the issue appealed to her in her roles as a political conservative fearful of the expansion of the federal government and as a religious conservative who believed that woman's obligation was to her family and that God had ordained for woman a submissive role. Unlike other conservative crusades, this one, Schlafly understood, "had to be fought and led by women."[7]

Out of the opposition to the ERA (and to abortion and other

single issues), a New Right coalition began to form. Orthodox Jews lobbied against a state referendum for the ERA in New York in 1975. Mormons joined the anti-ERA movement the following year. Protestant fundamentalist religious groups, especially in the South, were becoming interested. Schlafly had first developed her own political base out of an unsuccessful effort to gain the presidency of the National Federation of Republican Women. She went on to create a constituency of Republican women volunteers spread throughout her district in Illinois in her unsuccessful bid for Congress in 1970. These two groups formed the bulk of the readership of a newsletter she began to publish in 1967. She called on her readers to contribute to an independent trust fund she established in support of conservative causes. When she began to oppose the ERA in late 1972, she drew on her base of women supporters, her funding from this trust, and her knowledge of grassroots political organizing. Schlafly's leadership was crucial in forming a credible opposition; had there been no credible opposition, the ERA would not have been defeated.

It is difficult to decide whether Schlafly was an unusually skilled leader or the proponents of ERA were singularly uncharismatic. The leaders of the women's movement—Betty Friedan, Gloria Steinem, later Eleanor Smeal, perhaps even Shirley Chisholm and Bella Abzug—did not seem to generate the kind of dedicated following that Schlafly was able to attract. When a modern Carrie Chapman Catt was needed, there was none to be found. But Schlafly does have to be credited with proper management of her image. Even though both she and Smeal were homemakers in the technical sense (that is, they were mothers who did not earn wages, though both spent much of their time organizing their respective campaigns), Schlafly was able to appear as a representative of homemakers, whereas Smeal was perceived as a representative of "working women." Schlafly's supporters were as effective as she in appearing to be typical housewives lacking in political experience when they were, in fact, members of the radical or religious right with a long prior history of activism.[8]

The opponents of the ERA were able to slow the momentum in favor of the amendment, which helped them because time was on their side. The average constitutional amendment has been ratified by the states within eighteen months after passing Congress. The ERA began to die a slow death beginning in 1973. Only three states ratified the amendment in 1974, one in 1975, and one—the last—in 1977. In 1975, two northern liberal states, New York and New Jersey, both of which already had ratified the national amendment, placed on the ballot referenda concerning support for a state ERA. Voters in both states rejected the referenda. These losses proved to be major political upsets, because they suggested that despite favorable attitudes registered in public opinion polls, the voters did not actually support the ERA. There was only one more victory to come.

In 1979, Congress extended the deadline for ratification of the amendment by three more years. But more time would only prolong what had become a losing battle. With the exception of Schlafly's home state of Illinois, the others failing to ratify the ERA were states in the Deep South or the Rocky Mountain region. There was a striking resemblance between the opposition of these state legislatures to the ERA and their oposition to the woman's suffrage amendment. In these states, the opposition was concentrated among men of conservative views who represented rural districts. Bringing up the ERA year after year changed very few votes, and in some cases even stiffened the opposition.

One can always speculate about whether some dramatic strategy would have recaptured the momentum for the ERA and prompted its passage. The national boycott of unratified states, the decision to launch a national campaign rather than one concentrated in unratified states, and the millions of dollars spent on television advertising now appear to have been strat-

States which ratified ERA □

egies which did not work. Janet Boles, in a model of understate-
ment, writes that "there is an extraordinarily weak linkage between a commercial run on national television during prime
time and the vote of a Florida legislator."[9] If one looks at the
small groups of states where the ERA was passed either by
narrow margins or after several previous failures, it appears that
the fear of a women's bloc vote was the key to victory. But one
cannot reverse past events, as if history were a series of newsreels
waiting to be rewound. It is plausible to argue that by 1977 no
strategy would have led to victory.

The strategy of the opponents was to raise doubts about the
effect of the amendment. No one can predict in advance what
the future will bring. Who could have foreseen that the Fourteenth Amendment, designed to ensure the civil rights of ex-
slaves, would be reinterpreted by the courts to foster the interest
of large corporations? Experts on constitutional law predicted
the consequences of the ERA for American law, given the general pattern of judicial decisions in recent decades. But the
experts disagreed. For example, some claimed that the ERA
would furnish a constitutional argument to legalize marriage

between homosexuals, while others argued that it would not. All the opponents had to do was to create fear about the consequences of the ERA: women would be drafted; homosexual marriages would be legalized; alimony for divorced women would be disallowed. These were social changes which much of the public and many state legislators feared.

Opponents failed to make the ERA unpopular with the public; they did, however, succeed in making the public unsure about it. In Gallup polls, popular support for the ERA declined from 74 to 62 percent between 1974 and 1982. During these same years, the percentage of the public which did not know whether they favored the amendment rose from 5 to 15 percent.[10] By raising questions about the impact of the ERA on social policy in many areas, the opposition often succeeded in putting proponents of the ERA on the defensive, forcing them to spend time refuting the charges of the other side. The fact that opponents of the ERA were often not well organized was not a weakness but a strength, since it reinforced the male legislators' view of women as naive, helpless, and in need of protection. It also played into the attitude many legislators held that the demands of interest groups are illegitimate, whereas those of individuals are legitimate.

But the most important accomplishment of the opponents was that they succeeded in helping to transform the ERA from a nonpartisan, somewhat technical issue of constitutional law into a subject of great emotion and partisanship. There is little that politicians dislike as much as controversy. As proponents of the ERA in Georgia noted, "If we could have staged a quiet, behind-the-scenes campaign, we would have passed it."[11] When an issue becomes controversial, fair-weather friends begin to disappear, legislative sponsors back away, and party leaders become unwilling to compel their members to vote along party lines. Legislators dislike the disruption of normal routine which controversy brings. Many of them came to view the campaign as a contest between two opposing groups, equal in size and moral legitimacy. Votes ran along party lines in several states, or the ERA became enmeshed in state politics and personal feuds. Most of the legislators opposed to the ERA were males, and opposition was strongest among Republicans.[12]

Because the opponents of the ERA have become the winning side, it is easy to attribute to them greater political acumen than they in fact possessed. All they needed for victory was a one-vote plurality in one house in each of thirteen state legislatures. In order to win, they simply needed to present themselves as a credible opposition. The fairness doctrine of broadcasters permitted opponents to appear on radio and TV talk shows every time a proponent appeared. Schlafly was the titular leader of a highly decentralized movement whose real strength lay in local church groups.

The National Organization for Woman has alleged that right-wing foundations, the National Association of Manufacturers, and life insurance companies channeled vast sums of money into the anti-ERA campaign. (Insurance companies were opposed to the ERA because its passage might cut into their profits by forcing them to pay higher insurance benefits to women without being able to charge them higher premiums.) Women's suffrage was also opposed by business interests such as the liquor lobby, manufacturers' associations, and textile factory owners.[13] But one must also remember that vast sums of money were being spent in favor of the ERA, at least in the waning years of the campaign. In 1977, NOW was taking in $150,000 a year from ERA walkathons; by 1981, it was raising $1 million a year.[14] The only study to compare the funding of the two sides has been a tally of contributions to election campaigns for the Illinois state legislature.[15] In 1978, the one year for which information is available, opponents outspent proponents by only $6,000. Moreover, J. H. Jones argues that campaign contributions had some effect, though not substantial, on subsequent votes, which he believes were determined more by the social and political beliefs of the individual legislator.[16]

The longer the fight dragged on, the more doubts and fears surfaced about the nature of the amendment. The ERA seemed to be more popular the less people knew about it, which helps to explain why it fared so well at first in states which did not hold hearings or debates on it. As an issue, the ERA had the great disadvantage of touching on so many topics in law—crime, labor, family support, inheritance, and property rights—and on so many areas of public policy, such as the military and education. For the opponents, that was a great advantage, because they attracted adherents concerned with a single issue. Consider the Jewish mother who "decided to work against ratification of the ERA because if it were passed it would interfere with my son's right to keep an orthodox house." The opposition, thus, assembled a diverse coalition of "antis." They could disassociate the ERA from equal rights, which everyone favors, and associate it with the women's movement or gay liberation, which many do not favor. Opponents did not have to prove anything about the ERA: they merely had to generate doubts about it in the minds of legislators.

Opponents felt more strongly than proponents about the consequences of the ERA, because they had so much to fear, whereas proponents believed they had only a modest amount to gain. For women against the ERA, the amendment became a symbol of secular and sexual change threatening to undermine the traditional family by challenging laws requiring husbands to support the family and giving to women a favored position in divorce settlements. It was also claimed that with the passage of the ERA, a husband could force his wife to take a paying job and could compel her to bear her half of the financial support of the family.

These arguments expressed anxiety about changing male and female roles and the increased participation of women in the paid labor force. Trends as dramatic as these do not occur without engendering opponents who seek a return to the status quo or, more accurately, to an idealized version of the past. The women's movement, after all, had insisted that the personal was political. The female opponents of the ERA agreed and perceived the amendment as a symbol of changes in women's lives and in sexuality to which they were opposed. These changes represented a threat to their religious beliefs and their views about the proper role of women. The actual change in the Constitution which the ERA would have wrought became lost in the rhetoric in which the ERA figured as a symbol of undesired social change. But the confusion and lack of precision were not altogether unfair, since the proponents of the ERA tended to link the amendment with the ideal of equality and hope for greater results from ratification than could reasonably be expected.

But the desire of opponents to preserve the traditional family, an almost exact repetition of the arguments of the opponents of woman's suffrage, was only one of several objections to the ERA. For many military-minded state legislators, fear of drafting women and sending them into combat aroused protective feelings toward women and concern about the viability of the nation's defenses. Others were opposed to unnecessary intervention by the federal government and the federal judiciary in the rights of states. It was argued that because the amendment gave Congress the power to enforce the ERA, it would encroach upon the power of state legislatures. The image of a bloated federal bureaucracy grabbing power from states was one designed to strike fear in the hearts of state legislators, as Alice Paul always suspected.

Some of these arguments were simple repetitions of the states' rights arguments which surfaced during the effort to pass civil rights legislation on behalf of blacks, while others were more original and diverse concerns about unwieldy governmental bureaucracy and excessive invasion of privacy. This last type of argument—about the proper balance of power between the states and the federal government—has nothing to do with gender. Thus, the debate about the ERA ranged from proper definitions of woman's role to fears of military disaster and wariness toward governmental intervention in personal life.

State legislators also appear to have been convinced by the argument that the ERA was not needed. Had not women already been granted equal rights? The urgency of passing the ERA was undermined by the superficial appearance of equality created by the passage of so much federal legislation in the 1960s and early 1970s. In fact, the ERA was necessary not so much to legislate women's rights as to undergird these recent statutes, making their repeal more difficult and their interpretation by the courts less ambiguous. One saw quite a few yawns in the audience by the time proponents came to explain that the "suspect classification" test applied by the courts in cases of discrimination by race and religion was not generally followed in cases of sex discrimination. Since the constitutional experts often disagreed as to whether women's rights were protected under the Fourteenth Amendment, it was easy for the public and state legislators to become confused.

A major defeat cannot be sustained without affecting the movement which sponsored it. A fifty-nine-year struggle had come to an end, or at least to a long hiatus. The establishment core of the women's movement seemed to be narrowing on economic goals and rushing to shed controversial issues. But the more militant phase of the ratification campaign from 1977 to 1982 appears not to have weakened but to have strengthened the women's movement. Certainly the most concrete result was that the ERA helped attract members and funds to NOW. Traditional women's organizations, such as the Girl Scouts and the American Association of University Women, were brought into the women's movement coalition. By the end of the campaign, more than 450 organizations, with a total membership of fifty million, had gone on record in support of the ERA.[17]

NOW and national women's groups had their attention riveted on national politics in the early 1970s. The lesson they derived from the state campaigns for the ERA was to pay more attention to state and local politics by pouring funds and volunteers into supporting political candidates who favored their positions. Thus, the women's movement was both chastened and strengthened in defeat. Ultimately, the long campaign had proved that progress is not inevitable, that the initial wave of feminist enthusiasm is difficult to sustain, and that to secure women's rights will take renewed effort and determination.

Notes

1. Support for the ERA among women was highest among blacks, residents of the East Coast or large cities, those employed in clerical or sales jobs, and those who identified themselves as political moderates or liberals.

2. George Gallup, "Public Support for ERA Reaches New High," *Gallup Poll*, August 9, 1981, pp. 23–25.

3. *Gallup Poll*, August 9, 1981.

4. Janet K. Boles, *The Politics of the Equal Rights Amendment* (New York: Longman, 1979).

5. C. Mueller, "The Dramatic Reversal: Three Reasons for the Defeat of ERA" (unpublished paper, 1983).

6. C. Felsenthal, *The Sweetheart of the Silent Majority* (Garden City, N.J.: Doubleday, 1981), p. 240.

7. Lisa C. Wohl, "Phyllis Schlafly: 'The Sweetheart of the Silent Majority,'" *Ms.*, March 1974: 54–57, 85–89.

8. D. Brady and K. L. Tedin, "Ladies in Pink: Religion and Political Ideology in the Anti-ERA Movement," *Social Science Quarterly* 56 (March 1976): 564–75; K. L. Tedin, D. W. Brady, M. E. Buxton, B. M. Gorman, and J. L. Thompson, "Religious Preference and Pro-Anti Activism on the Equal Rights Amendment Issue," *Pacific Sociological Review* 21 (1978): 55–66; K. L. Tedin, D. W. Brady, M. E. Buxton, B. M. Gorman, and J. L. Thompson, "Social Background and Political Differences between Pro- and Anti-ERA Activists," *American Politics Quarterly* 5 (1977): 395–408.

9. Janet K. Boles, "Building Support for the ERA: A Case of 'Too Much Too Late,'" *Political Science* 15 (Fall 1982): 576.

10. M. R. Daniels, R. Darcy, and J. W. Westphal, "The ERA Won—At Least in the Opinion Polls," *Political Science* 15 (Fall 1982): 578–84.

11. Boles, *Politics of the Equal Rights Amendment*, pp. 134–38.

12. J. R. Lilie, R. Handberg, Jr., and W. Lowrey, "Women State

Legislators and the ERA: Dimensions of Support and Opposition," *Women and Politics* 2 (1–2): 23–38.

13. Eleanor Flexner, *Century of Struggle: The Woman's Rights Movement in the United States* (New York: Atheneum, 1968).

14. Boles, "Building Support for the ERA," p. 574.

15. J. H. Jones, "The Effect of the Pro- and Anti-ERA Campaign Contributions on the ERA Voting Behavior of Eightieth Illinois House of Representatives," *Women in Politics* 2, nos. 1–2 (Spring–Summer 1982) 71–86.

16. I. E. Deutchman and S. Prince-Embury, "Political Ideology of Pro- and Anti-ERA Women," *Women and Politics* 2, nos. 1–2 (Spring–Summer 1982) 39–55.

17. Boles, "Building Support for the ERA," pp. 572–77.

Appendix: Various Attempts to Define Equal Rights for Women

Original Equal Rights Amendment, 1923:

Men and women shall have equal rights throughout the United States and every place subject to its jurisdiction.

Congress shall have power to enforce this article by appropriate legislation.

From The Women's Charter, 1936 (to counter ERA):

Women shall [have] full political and civil rights; full opportunity for education, full opportunity for work according to their individual abilities, with safeguards against physically harmful conditions of employment and economic exploitation. They shall receive compensation, without discrimination because of sex. They shall be assured security of livelihood, including the safeguarding of motherhood. The provisions necessary for the establishment of these standards shall be guaranteed by government, which shall insure also the right of united action towards the attainment of these aims. Where special exploitation of women workers exists, such as low wages which provide less than the living standards attainable, unhealthful working conditions or long hours of work which result in physical exhaustion and denial of the right to leisure, such conditions shall be corrected through social and labor legislation, which the world's experience shows to be necessary.

Senator Harley Kilgore's (D., West Virginia) version, 1943:

Equality of rights under the law shall not be denied or abridged by the United States or by any State on account of sex.

Congress and the several States shall have power, within their respective jurisdictions, to enforce this article by appropriate legislation.

This amendment shall not require uniformity of legislation among the several States, the District of Columbia, the Territories, and possessions of the United States.

Senator Warren Austin's (R., Vermont) version, 1943:

Equality of rights under the law shall not be denied or abridged by the United States or by any State on account of sex.

Congress and the several States shall have power, within their respective jurisdictions, to enforce this article by appropriate legislation.

This amendment shall take effect five years after the date of ratification.

The United Automobile, Aircraft, and Agriculture Implement Workers of America's suggested rider, 1945:

. . . Nothing in this article shall be construed as to invalidate or prevent legislation improving the working conditions of women.

The Committee of American Women, affiliate group of the Women's International Democratic Federation, suggested amendment, 1945:

There shall be no economic, legal, political, or social discrimination because of sex or marital status in the United States of America or Territory subject to its jurisdiction. Nothing in this article shall be so construed as to invalidate or prevent enactment of legislation benefiting women in their work or family status.

Senator Richard Russell's (D., Georgia) proposed rider:

. . . This article shall be inoperative unless it shall have been ratified as an amendment to the Constitution by the legislatures of three-fourths of the several States within five years from the date of its submission to the States by the Congress; and if so ratified, shall take effect upon the expiration of one year after the date of such ratification.

ERA with rider added by Senator Carl Hayden (D., Arizona), passed by U.S. Senate on 25 January, 1950 and 16 July, 1953:

Equality of rights under the law shall not be denied or abridged by the United States or by any State on account of sex.

The provisions of this article shall not be construed to impair any rights, benefits, or exemptions now or hereafter conferred by law upon persons of the female sex.

The Congress and the several States shall have power, within their respective jurisdictions, to enforce this article by appropriate legislation.

This article shall be inoperative unless it shall have been ratified as an amendment to the Constitution by the legislatures of three-fourths of the several States within seven years from the date of its submission to the States by the Congress; and if so ratified, shall take effect upon the expiration of one year after the date of such ratification.

Kefauver women's status-bill, proposed as a substitute for the Equal Rights Amendment in the Eighty-first Congress, second session, 1950:

A Bill To provide for the investigation of discriminations against women on the basis of sex, to establish policies for the removal of such discriminations, and for other purposes.

Whereas the economic, civil, social, and political progress of women has been burdened and impeded by discriminations arising in part from assumptions embedded in the common law; and

Whereas notwithstanding notable legislative achievements in modern times, there remain in effect statutes, regulations, rules, and governmental practices which discriminate unfairly on the basis of sex; and

Whereas the authority and jurisdiction to remove existing burdens and impediments upon the status of women resides, to a great extent, in the legislatures of the several States; and

Whereas the present is an appropriate occasion to review the political, civil, economic, and social status of women for the purpose of modernizing applicable legal codes and administrative practices: Now therefore,

Be it enacted by the Senate and House of Representatives of the United States of America in Congress Assembled, That it is the declared policy of the United States that in law and its administration no distinctions on the basis of sex shall be made except such as are reasonably justified by differences in physical structure, or by maternal function.

Wadsworth-Taft women's status-bill, proposed in the Eightieth Congress, second session, 1950:

A Bill To establish a commission on the legal status of women in the United States, to declare a policy as to distinctions based on sex, in law and administration, and for other purposes

Whereas the economic, civil, social, and political progress of women has been burdened and impeded by discriminations arising in part from assumptions embedded in common law; and

Whereas notwithstanding notable legislative achievements in modern times there remain in effect statutes, regulations, rules, and governmental practices which discriminate unfairly on the basis of sex; and

Whereas since the Charter of the United Nations, ratified by and for the United States on July 28, 1945, declares it to be among its purposes to 'achieve international cooperation in . . . promoting and encouraging respect for human rights and fundamental freedoms for all without distinctions as to . . . sex' (art. 1), it should be the purpose of the United States and several States and their political subdivisions, to bring their laws and the administration thereof into harmony with these principles; and

Whereas the authority and jurisdiction to remove existing burdens and implements upon the status of women resides, to a great extent, in the legislatures of the several States; and

Whereas the present is an appropriate occasion to review the political, civil, economic, and social status of women for the purpose of modernizing applicable legal codes and administrative practices: Now therefore

Be it enacted by the Senate and House of Representatives of the United States of America in Congress assembled, That it is the declared policy of the United States that in law and its administration no distinctions on the basis of sex shall be made except such as are reasonably justified by differences in physical structure, biological, or social function.

Helen Hill Weed's suggested rider, 1950:

. . . The provisions of this article shall not be construed to invalidate special legislation conferring benefits or exemptions on legally defined classes of men and women.

Alice Paul's suggested rider, 1950:

. . . This article shall not be construed to impair any rights, benefits, exemptions, or protection conferred upon men and women equally, or conferred upon one sex alone when inapplicable to both sexes.

Ethel Ernest Murrell's suggested rider, 1950:

. . . This article shall not be construed to impair any rights, benefits, exemptions, or protection conferred upon men and women equally or conferred upon one sex alone when inapplicable to both sexes, or any special consideration given to women on grounds of motherhood.

Olive B. Lacy's suggested rider, 1950:

. . . This article shall not be construed to impair any benefits or exemptions now or hereafter conferred especially upon one sex or the other because inapplicable to both sexes.

Senate Joint Resolution, 1953:

. . . an amendment to the Constitution of the United States, to assure the equal application thereof to individuals of both sexes.

Resolved by the Senate and House of Representatives of the United

States of America in Congress assembled (two-thirds of each house concurring therein), That the following article is hereby proposed as an amendment to the Constitution of the United States, which shall be valid to all intents and purposes as part of the Constitution when ratified by the legislatures of three-fourths of the several States:

ARTICLE

Section 1. Whenever in this Constitution the term 'person, persons, people,' or any personal pronoun is used the same shall be taken to include both sexes.

Section 2. All Federal and State laws inconsistent herewith shall be deemed amended to conform hereto when this article shall take effect; and, the Congress and the several States shall have concurrent power, within their respective jurisdictions, to enforce this article by appropriate legislation.

Final Equal Rights Amendment, 1972:

Section 1. Equality of rights under the law shall not be denied or abridged by the United States or by any State on account of sex.

Section 2. The Congress shall have the power to enforce, by appropriate legislation, the provisions of this article.

Section 3. This amendment shall take effect two years after the date of ratification.

Bibliography

Alexander, Shana. *State-by-State Guide to Women's Legal Rights*. Los Angeles: Wollstonecraft, 1975.

"The American Woman." *Trans-action* 8, nos. 1–2 (November/December 1970).

"Answering Opponents of Equal Rights." *Independent Woman* 26 (October 1947): 302.

Anthony, Susan B. "The 'Equal Rights' Amendment; An Attack on Labor." *Lawyer's Guild Review*, January 1943, pp. 12–17.

Babcock, Barbara Allen; Freedman, Ann E.; Norton, Eleanor Holmes; and Ross, Susan C. *Sex Discrimination and the Law: Causes and Remedies*. Boston: Little, Brown and Co., 1975.

Baer, Judith A. *The Chains of Protection: The Judicial Response to Women's Labor Legislation*. Westport, Conn.: Greenwood Press, 1978.

———. *Equality under the Constitution: Reclaiming the Fourteenth Amendment*. Ithaca, N.Y.: Cornell University Press, 1983.

Banks, Olive. *Faces of Feminism: A Study of Feminism as a Social Movement*. New York: St. Martin's Press, 1981.

Becker, Susan D. *The Origins of the Equal Rights Amendment: American Feminism between the Wars*. Westport, Conn.: Greenwood Press, 1981.

Berry, Mary Frances. *Why ERA Failed*. Bloomington: Indiana University Press, 1986.

Blahna, Loretta J. "The Rhetoric of the Equal Rights Amendment." Ph.D. dissertation, University of Kansas, 1973.

Boles, Janet K. "Building Support for the ERA: A Case of 'Too Much Too Late.'" *Political Science* 15 (Fall 1982).

———. "The Coalescence of Controversy: Conditions Surrounding Ratification of the Proposed Equal Rights Amendment." Ph.D. dissertation, University of Texas at Austin, 1976.

———. *The Politics of the Equal Rights Amendment*. New York: Longman, 1979.

Brady, David W., and Tedin, Kent L. "Ladies in Pink: Religion and Political Ideology in the Anti-ERA Movement." *Social Science Quarterly* 56 (March 1976): 564–75.

Brown, Barbara A.; Emerson, Thomas I.; Falk, Gail; and Freedman, Ann E. "The Equal Rights Amendment: A Constitutional Basis for Equal Rights for Women." *Yale Law Journal* 80 (April 1971): 871–985.

Brown, Dorothy. *Mabel Walker Willebrandt: A Study of Power, Loyalty, and Law.* Knoxville: University of Tennessee Press, 1984.

Campbell, Karlyn Kohrs. "The Rhetoric of Women's Liberation: An Oxymoron." *Quarterly Journal of Speech* 59 (February 1973): 74–86.

Chafe, William H. *The American Woman: Her Changing Social, Economic, and Political Role, 1920–1970.* New York: Oxford University Press, 1972.

———. *Women and Equality: Changing Patterns in American Culture.* New York: Oxford University Press, 1978.

Clark, Barbara A. "The Rhetoric of Women's Rights: A Study of the Controversy Surrounding the Proposed Equal Rights Amendment." Master's thesis, University of Kansas, 1973.

Congressional Record, July 18, 1946, pp. 9225, 9401.

Congressional Record, March 7, 1950, p. A2054.

Congressional Record, September 10, 1970, p. 31132.

Congressional Record, March 2, 1972, p. 6765.

Congressional Record, March 28, 1972, p. 10450–56.

Coussins, Jean. *Equality Report.* London: National Council for Civil Liberties, 1977.

Crable, E. C. "Pros and Cons of the Equal Rights Amendment." *Women Lawyers Journal* 35 (Summer 1949): 7–9.

Daniels, M. R.; Darey, R.; and Westphal, J. W. "The ERA Won—At Least in the Opinion Polls." *Political Science* 15 (Fall 1982): 578–84.

Davidson, Kenneth; Ginsburg, Ruth Bader; and Kay, Herma Hill. *Text, Cases, and Materials on Sex-Based Discrimination.* St. Paul, Minn.: West Publishing Co., 1974.

Deckard, Barbara Sinclair. *The Women's Movement: Political, Socioeconomic, and Psychological Issues.* New York: Harper and Row, 1975.

DeCrow, Karen. *Sexist Justice.* New York: Vintage Books, 1975.

Defeis, Elizabeth F. *Women and the Law: A Video Course in Color.* Newark, N.J.: Seton Hall University School of Law.

Deutchman, I. E., and Prince-Embury, S. "Political Ideology of Pro- and Anti-ERA Women." *Women and Politics* 2, nos. 1–2 (Spring–Summer 1982) 39–55.

Dorsen, Norma, and Ross, Susan Deller, "The Necessity of a Constitutional Amendment." *Harvard Civil Rights-Civil Liberties Law Review* 6 (March 1971): 216–24.

Dunshee, Esther. "Miss Dunshee on 'Equal Rights.'" *Woman Citizen,* March 1924, p. 19.

Eastwood, Mary. "The Double Standard of Justice: Women's Rights under the Constitution." *Valparaiso University Law Review* 5 (1971): 281–317.

Epstein, Cynthia Fuchs. *Women in Law.* New York: Basic Books, 1982.

"Equality of Women." *America* 109 (October 26, 1963): 473.

"Equal Rights." *Women's Home Companion,* April 1939, p. 2.

"Equal Rights Amendment." *Ave Maria* 65 (February 1, 1947): 133.
"Equal Rights Amendment." *Social Justice Review* 37 (March 1945): 383–84.
"Equal Rights Amendment and the Woman Worker." *Catholic Action* 25 (February 1943): 18.
"The Equal Rights Amendment: Is It the Next Step to Women's Freedom?" *Graduate Woman* 47 (October 1953): 20–27.
"Equal Rights for Women?" *New Republic* 94 (February 16, 1938): 34.
"Equal Rights for Women: A Symposium on the Proposed Constitutional Amendment." *Harvard Civil Rights-Civil Liberties Law Review* 6 (March 1971): 215–87.
"Equal Rights for Women? Things May Never Be the Same." *U.S. News and World Report* 69 (August 24, 1970): 29–30.
"Equal Rights for Women Workers; A New Push." *U.S. News and World Report* 69 (August 3, 1970): 51–52.
"Equal Rights NOW." *Newsweek* 75 (March 2, 1970): 75.
Felsenthal, C. *The Sweetheart of the Silent Majority.* Garden City, N.J.: Doubleday, 1981.
Flexner, Eleanor. *Century of Struggle: The Woman's Rights Movement in the United States.* New York: Atheneum, 1968.
Forbus, Lady Willie. "The Lucretia Mott Amendment." *Equal Rights,* April 26, 1924, p. 85.
Foss, Karen Ann. "Ideological Manifestations in the Discourse of Contemporary Feminism." Ph.D. dissertation, University of Iowa, 1976.
Foss, Sonja Kay. "A Fantasy Theme Analysis of the Rhetoric of the Debate on the Equal Rights Amendment, 1970–1976: Toward a Theory of the Rhetoric of Movements." Ph.D. dissertation, Northwestern University, 1976.
———. "The Equal Rights Amendment Controversy: Two Worlds in Conflict." *Quarterly Journal of Speech* 65, no. 3 (1979): 275–88.
Freeman, Jo. *The Politics of Women's Liberation.* New York: David McKay and Co., 1975.
———. "The Politics of Women's Liberation: A Case Study of an Emerging Social Movement and Its Relation to the Policy Process." Ph.D. dissertation, State University of New York at Old Westbury, 1973.
Freund, Paul. "The Equal Rights Amendment Is Not the Way." *Harvard Civil Rights-Civil Liberties Law Review* 6 (March 1971): 234–42.
Fry, Amelia R. *Conversations with Alice Paul.* Oral history prepared for the Regional Oral History Office, the Bancroft Library, University of California, Berkeley, 1972–73.
Frye, Jerry K. *FIND: Frye's Index to Nonverbal Data.* Duluth: University of Minnesota Computer Center, 1980.
Gallup, George. "Public Support for the ERA Reaches New High." *Gallup Poll,* August 9, 1981.
Ginsburg, Ruth Bader. "The Need for the Equal Rights Amendment."

American Bar Association Journal 59 (September 1973): 1013–29.

Glynn, Edward. "How to Unnerve Male Chauvinists." *America* 123 (September 12, 1970): 144–46; 123 (October 10, 1970): 247.

Goldstein, Leslie Frieman. *The Constitutional Rights of Women.* New York: Longman, 1979.

Greathouse, Rebekah S. "The Effect of Constitutional Equality on Working Women." *American Economic Review,* Supplement (March 1944), pp. 227–36.

Greenberg, Hazel, and Miller, Anita, eds. *The Equal Rights Amendment: A Bibliographic Study.* Westport, Conn.: Greenwood Press, 1976.

Guggenheim, Malvina H., and Defeis, Elizabeth F. "United States Participation in International Agreements Providing Rights for Women." 10 *Loyola Law Review* 1 (1976): 1–71.

Hale, Judith, and Levine, Ellen. *Rebirth of Feminism.* New York: Quadrangle Books, 1971.

Hamilton, Alice. "The 'Blanket' Amendment—A Debate—Protection for Women Workers." *Forum* 72 (August 1924): 152–60.

Harris, Louis. "Public Support for ERA Soars as Ratification Deadline Nears." *Harris Survey,* May 6, 1982.

———. "Support Increasing for Strengthening Women's Status in Society." *Harris Survey,* August 17, 1981.

Helmes, Winifred. "Equal Rights, Where Do We Stand?" *Graduate Woman* 46 (March 1953): 165.

Hill, Anne Corinne. "Protection of Women Workers and the Courts: A Legal Case History." *Feminist Studies* 5, no. 2 (Summer 1979): 247–73.

Hoff-Wilson, Joan. *Balancing the Scales: Changing Legal Status of American Women.* Bloomington: Indiana University Press, forthcoming.

———. "Women and the Constitution." APSA *Newsletter,* no. 46 (Summer 1985), pp. 10–16.

Hornaday, M. "Showdown on Equal Rights: Amending the Constitution." *Christian Science Monitor,* October 9, 1943, p. 5.

House of Representatives. *Hearings on ERA,* 1945.

Huber, Joan et al. "A Crucible of opinion on Women's Status: ERA in Illinois." *Social Forces* 57 (December 1978): 549–65.

"'I Didn't Raise My Girl to Be a Soldier': Sense and Nonsense about the ERA." *Christian Century,* October 25, 1972, pp. 1056–58.

Irwin, Inez Haynes. "Why the Woman's Party Is for It." *Good Housekeeping,* March 1924, p. 18.

Jones, J. H. "The Effect of the Pro- and Anti-ERA Campaign Contributions on the ERA Voting of Behavior of Eightieth Illinois House Representatives." *Women in Politics* 2, nos. 1–2 (Spring–Summer 1982): 71–86.

Kelley, Florence. "The New Woman's Party." *Survey* 45 (March 5, 1921): 827.

————. "Why Other Women's Groups Oppose It." *Good Housekeeping*, March 1924, p. 19.

————, comp. "Twenty Questions about the Federal Amendment Proposed by the National Woman's Party." New York: National Consumers' League, 1922.

Kenton, E. "Ladies' Next Step: The Case for the Equal Rights Amendment." *Harper's* 152 (February 1926): 366–74.

Kraditor, Aileen, ed. *Up from the Pedestal: Selected Writings in the History of American Feminism*. Chicago: Quadrangle Books, 1970.

Krichmar, Albert. *The Women's Rights Movement in the United States, 1848–1970: A Bibliography and Source Book*. Metuchen, N.J.: Scarecrow Press, 1972.

Kurland, Philip B. "The Equal Rights Amendment: Some Problems of Construction." *Harvard Civil Rights-Civil Liberties Law Review* 6 (March 1971): 243–52.

"Ladies' Day." *Newsweek* 76 (August 24, 1970): 15–16.

Lee, Rex E. *A Lawyer Looks at the Equal Rights Amendment*. Provo: Brigham Young University, 1980.

Lemons, J. Stanley. *The Woman Citizen: Social Feminism in the 1920s*. Urbana: University of Illinois Press, 1973.

"Letter to the Senate," S.J. Res. 61, July 18, 1946. *Congressional Record* 42, p. 9401.

Lilie, J. R.; Handberg, R. Jr.; and Lowrey, W. "Women State Legislators and the ERA: Dimensions of Support and Opposition." *Women and Politics* 2, nos. 1–2 (Spring–Summer 1982) 23–38.

Lutz, Alma. "Only One Choice." *Independent Woman*, July 1947, pp. 199–205.

————. "Why Bar Equality?" *Christian Science Monitor*, July 22, 1944, p. 3.

Mansbridge, Jane. *Why We Lost the ERA*. Chicago: University of Chicago Press, 1986.

Mathews, Jane DeHart. "The ERA and the Myth of Female Solidarity." American Historical Association, paper, December 1983.

Mayo, Edith P. "The Battle's Not Over: ERA, 1923–1982." *Keynoter* 82, no. 3: 18–25.

"Men and Women: Equality or Equity?" *America* 123 (September 19, 1970): 167–68.

Meyer, Carol Finn. "Attitudes toward the Equal Rights Amendment." Ph.D. dissertation, City University of New York, 1979.

Murray, Pauli. "The Negro Woman's Stake in the Equal Rights Amendment." *Harvard Civil Rights-Civil Liberties Law Review* 6 (March 1971): 253–59.

National Organizaton for Women. "Bill of Rights for 1969." Reprinted in *Herstory: A Woman's View of American History*, ed. June Sochen, pp. 435–36. New York: Alfred Publishing Co., 1974.

"New Victory in an Old Crusade." *Time* 96 (August 24, 1970): 10–12.

"Next Step in the Emancipation of Women—An Equal Rights Amendment?" *Graduate Woman* 31 (April 1938): 160–64.

Offen, Karen. "Toward an Historical Definition of Feminism: The Contribution of France." Center for Research on Women working paper no. 22. Stanford University.

Ondercin, David George. "The Complete Woman: The Equal Rights Amendment and Perceptions of Womanhood, 1920–1972." Ph.D. dissertation, University of Minnesota, 1973.

O'Neill, William L. *The Woman Movement: Feminism in the United States and England.* London: George Allen and Unwin, 1969.

"Organizations Supporting the Equal Rights Amendment." *National NOW Times,* May 13, 1980.

Paul, Alice. *Congressional Record* 20 (April 1943): 107.

Peak, Mayme Ober. "Women in Politics." *Outlook* 136 (January 23, 1924): 147–50.

Portnow, Billie. "What's Wrong with the Equal Rights Amendment?" *Jewish Currents* 25 (July/August 1971): 4–9.

Puller, Edwin S. "When Equal Rights Are Unequal." *Virginia Law Review* 13 (June 1927): 619–30.

Purcell, Susan Kaufman. "Ideology and the Law: Sexism and the Supreme Court Decisions." In *Women in Politics,* ed. Jane Jaquette. New York: John Wiley and Sons, 1974.

Randall, Susan Louise. "A Legislative History of the Equal Rights Amendment, 1923–1960." Ph.D. dissertation, University of Utah, 1979.

"Rights for Women." *Newsweek,* July 29, 1946, p. 17.

Robinson, Donald Allen. "Two Movements in Pursuit of Equal Opportunities." *Signs* 4 (Spring 1979): 413–33.

Ross, Susan C. *The Rights of Women: The Basic ACLU Guide to a Woman's Rights.* New York: Sunshine Books, 1973.

Scharf, Lois. *Female Employment Feminism and the Great Depression.* Westport, Conn.: Greenwood Press, 1980.

Schlafly, Phyllis. "The Case against ERA." *Radcliffe Quarterly* 68 (March 1982): 18–20.

Schlafly Report 5, no. 7 (February 1972).

Schlafly Report 9, no. 11 (June 1976).

Sex Bias in the United States Code: A Report of the U.S. Commission on Civil Rights. Washington, D.C.: Government Printing Office, April 1977.

Sherrill, R. "That Equal Rights Amendment: What Exactly Does It Mean?" *New York Times Magazine,* September 20, 1970, pp. 25–27.

Smith, Ethel M. "Equal Rights and Equal Rights: What Is Wrong with the Woman's Party Amendment?" Chicago: National Women's Trade Union League of America [1925?].

Smith-Rosenberg, Carroll. *Disorderly Conduct: Visions of Gender in Victorian America.* New York: Knopf, 1985.

✓Solomon, Martha. "The Rhetoric of STOP ERA: Fatalistic Reaffirmation." *Southern Speech Communication Journal* 44, no. 1 (1978): 42–59.
Speiner, Gilbert. *Constitutional Inequality: The Political Fortunes of the Equal Rights Amendment*. Washington, D.C.: Brookings Institution Press, 1985.
Stevens, Doris. "The 'Blanket' Amendment—A Debate: Suffrage Does Not Give Equality." *Forum* 60, no. 12 (August 1924): 151.
Tedin, Kent L. "If the Equal Rights Amendment Becomes Law: Perceptions of Consequences among Female Activists and Masses." Midwest Political Science Association, paper, 1980.
Tedin, K. L.; Brady, D. W.; Buxton, M. E.; Gorman, B. M.; and Thompson, J. L. "Religious Preference and Pro-Anti Activism on the Equal Rights Amendment Issue." *Pacific Sociological Review* 21 (1978): 55–66.
———. "Social Background and Political Differences between Pro- and Anti-ERA Activists." *American Politics Quarterly* 5 (1977): 395–408.
Temple, M. L. "Is Your Representative among Those Present?" *Independent Woman* 33 (June 1954): 223–24.
United States Citizens Advisory Council on the Status of Women. "Report of the Committee on Civil and Political Rights." Washington, D.C.: Government Printing Office, 1963.
Williams, Wendy W. "The Equality Crisis: Some Reflections on Culture, Courts, and Feminism." *Women's Rights Law Reporter* 7, no. 3 (Spring 1982): 175–200.
✓Wohl, Lisa Cronin. "Phyllis Schlafly: The Sweetheart of the Silent Majority." *Ms.*, March 1974, pp. 55–57, 85–89.
———. "White Gloves and Combat Boots: The Fight for ERA." *Civil Liberties Review* 1 (Fall 1974): 77–86.
Yates, Gayle Graham. *What Women Want: The Ideas of the Women's Movement*. Cambridge, Mass.: Harvard University Press, 1975.

Contributors

JANET K. BOLES, Assistant Professor of Political Science and Codirector of the Institute for Citizenship and Public Policy at Marquette University, is the author of *The Politics of the Equal Rights Amendment* and is currently editing *The Egalitarian City.* Her articles on family policy, the ERA, women and politics, and urban neighborhoods have appeared in journals and edited books.

BERENICE A. CARROLL is Director of Women's Studies and Associate Professor of Political Science at the University of Illinois at Urbana-Champaign. She is author of *Design for Total War: Arms and Economics in the Third Reich,* editor and coauthor of *Liberating Women's History: Theoretical and Critical Essays,* and author of many articles, essays, and other works. She has served as editor of *Peace and Change: A Journal of Peace Research,* and has been active in various branches of the peace movement and the women's movement. Her current research interests focus on the history of women's political thought and on the theory of feminism and pacifism.

ELIZABETH F. DEFEIS is Professor of Law and Dean at Seton Hall Law Center. Among her publications are several articles dealing with women's rights, including "United States Participation in International Agreements Providing Rights for Women" and "The Fourteenth Amendment: A Century of Law and History."

JANE DeHART-MATHEWS is Professor of History and American Studies and Director of Women's Studies at the University of North Carolina at Chapel Hill. She is currently working with

Donald G. Mathews on a study of the ratification struggle, *The Equal Rights Amendment and the Politics of Cultural Conflict*, from which the essay in this volume is based. Her recent book, *Women's America: Refocusing the Past*, was coauthored with Linda K. Kerber.

AMELIA R. FRY is project director of the California Governmental Eras oral history series and interviewer-editor of the suffragist series at the Regional Oral History Office at the University of California at Berkeley. She is working on a biography of Alice Paul and has written several papers and articles on Paul's life and campaigns.

JERRY K. FRYE, Associate Professor of Mass Communication at the University of Minnesota, Duluth, is the author of *FIND: Frye's Index to Nonverbal Data*, as well as several communication textbooks and numerous articles for scholarly publications. Dr. Frye is currently a Research Fellow at the Smithsonian Institution's National Museum of American History.

JOAN HOFF-WILSON, Executive Secretary of the Organization of American Historians and Professor of History at Indiana University, is author of the Bernath Prize book *American Business and Foreign Policy, 1920–1933; Ideology and Economics: United States Relations with the Soviet Union, 1918–1933;* and *Herbert Hoover: Forgotten Progressive;* and coauthor of *Sexism and the Law: Male Beliefs and Legal Bias in Britain and the United States.*

DONALD G. MATHEWS, on the faculty at the University of North Carolina at Chapel Hill, is a social historian with articles and books on religion in American life including *Religion in the Old South.* He is currently writing a book with Jane DeHart-Mathews titled *ERA and the Politics of Cultural Conflict.*

EDITH P. MAYO, Curator and Supervisor of the Division of Political History, National Museum of American History, Smithsonian Institution, has written, lectured, and collected in the fields of women's history, material culture, and civil rights and voting reform.

ELIZABETH PLECK is a Research Associate at the Center for Research on Women, Wellesley College, and Project Historian with the Public Media Foundation of Boston. She is developing a college-level audiocourse on the History of Women and the Family in America, 1607–1864. She is one of the coauthors of the OAH publication *Restoring Women to History: US History II*.

KATHRYN KISH SKLAR is Professor of History at the University of California, Los Angeles, where she teaches the history of American women. Her current research focuses on Florence Kelley and the women's world of Progressive reform, 1880–1930.

Index